# COMMON CORE MATHEMATICS

## NEW YORK EDITION

## Grade 2, Module 2: Addition and Subtraction of Length Units

## JB JOSSEY-BASS™

A Wiley Brand

Cover design by Chris Clary

Published by Jossey-Bass
A Wiley Brand
One Montgomery Street, Suite 1200, San Francisco, CA 94104-4594—www.josseybass.com

ISBN: 978-1-118-79363-3

Printed in the United States of America
FIRST EDITION
*PB Printing*      10  9  8  7  6  5  4  3  2  1

# WELCOME

Dear Teacher,

Thank you for your interest in Common Core's curriculum in mathematics. Common Core is a non-profit organization based in Washington, DC dedicated to helping K-12 public schoolteachers use the power of high-quality content to improve instruction.[1] We are led by a board of master teachers, scholars, and current and former school, district, and state education leaders. Common Core has responded to the Common Core State Standards' (CCSS) call for "content-rich curriculum"[2] by creating new, CCSS-based curriculum materials in mathematics, English Language Arts, history, and (soon) the arts. All of our materials are written by teachers who are among the nation's foremost experts on the new standards.

In 2012 Common Core won three contracts from the New York State Education Department to create a PreKindergarten–12th grade mathematics curriculum for the teachers of that state, and to conduct associated professional development. The book you hold contains a portion of that work. In order to respond to demand in New York and elsewhere, modules of the curriculum will continue to be published, on a rolling basis, as they are completed. This curriculum is based on New York's version of the CCSS (the CCLS, or Common Core Learning Standards). Common Core will be releasing an enhanced version of the curriculum this summer on our website, commoncore.org. That version also will be published by Jossey-Bass, a Wiley brand.

Common Core's curriculum materials are not merely aligned to the new standards, they take the CCSS as their very foundation. Our work in math takes its shape from the expectations embedded in the new standards— including the instructional shifts and mathematical progressions, and the new expectations for student fluency, deep conceptual understanding, and application to real-life context. Similarly, our ELA and history curricula are deeply informed by the CCSS's new emphasis on close reading, increased use of informational text, and evidence-based writing.

Our curriculum is distinguished not only by its adherence to the CCSS. The math curriculum is based on a theory of teaching math that is proven to work. That theory posits that mathematical knowledge is most coherently and

---

1. Despite the coincidence of name, Common Core and the Common Core State Standards are not affiliated. Common Core was established in 2007, prior to the start of the Common Core State Standards Initiative, which was led by the National Governors Association and the Council for Chief State School Officers.
2. *Common Core State Standards for English Language Arts & Literacy in History/Social Studies, Science, and Technical Subjects* (Washington, DC: Common Core State Standards Initiative), 6.

effectively conveyed when it is taught in a sequence that follows the "story" of mathematics itself. This is why we call the elementary portion of this curriculum "The Story of Units," to be followed by "The Story of Ratios" in middle school, and "The Story of Functions" in high school. Mathematical concepts flow logically, from one to the next, in this curriculum. The sequencing has been joined with methods of instruction that have been proven to work, in this nation and abroad. These methods drive student understanding beyond process, to deep mastery of mathematical concepts. The goal of the curriculum is to produce students who are not merely literate, but fluent, in mathematics.

It is important to note that, as extensive as these curriculum materials are, they are not meant to be prescriptive. Rather, they are intended to provide a basis for teachers to hone their own craft through study, collaboration, training, and the application of their own expertise as professionals. At Common Core we believe deeply in the ability of teachers and in their central and irreplaceable role in shaping the classroom experience. We strive only to support and facilitate their important work.

The teachers and scholars who wrote these materials are listed beginning on the next page. Their deep knowledge of mathematics, of the CCSS, and of what works in classrooms defined this work in every respect. I would like to thank Louisiana State University professor of mathematics Scott Baldridge for the intellectual leadership he provides to this project. Teacher, trainer, and writer Robin Ramos is the most inspired math educator I've ever encountered. It is Robin and Scott's aspirations for what mathematics education in America *should* look like that is spelled out in these pages.

Finally, this work owes a debt to project director Nell McAnelly that is so deep I'm confident it never can be repaid. Nell, who leads LSU's Gordon A. Cain Center for STEM Literacy, oversees all aspects of our work for NYSED. She has spent days, nights, weekends, and many cancelled vacations toiling in her efforts to make it possible for this talented group of teacher-writers to produce their best work against impossible deadlines. I'm confident that in the years to come Scott, Robin, and Nell will be among those who will deserve to be credited with putting math instruction in our nation back on track.

Thank you for taking an interest in our work. Please join us at www.commoncore.org.

Lynne Munson
President and Executive Director
Common Core
Washington, DC
June 20, 2013

## Common Core's K-5 Math Staff

Scott Baldridge, Lead Mathematician and Writer
Robin Ramos, Lead Writer, PreKindergarten-5
Jill Diniz, Lead Writer, 6-12
Ben McCarty, Mathematician

Nell McAnelly, Project Director
Tiah Alphonso, Associate Director
Jennifer Loftin, Associate Director
Catriona Anderson, Curriculum Manager,
    PreKindergarten-5

Sherri Adler, PreKindergarten
Debbie Andorka-Aceves, PreKindergarten

Kate McGill Austin, Kindergarten
Nancy Diorio, Kindergarten
Lacy Endo-Peery, Kindergarten
Melanie Gutierrez, Kindergarten
Nuhad Jamal, Kindergarten
Cecilia Rudzitis, Kindergarten
Shelly Snow, Kindergarten

Beth Barnes, First Grade
Lily Cavanaugh, First Grade
Ana Estela, First Grade
Kelley Isinger, First Grade
Kelly Spinks, First Grade
Marianne Strayton, First Grade
Hae Jung Yang, First Grade

Wendy Keehfus-Jones, Second Grade
Susan Midlarsky, Second Grade
Jenny Petrosino, Second Grade
Colleen Sheeron, Second Grade
Nancy Sommer, Second Grade
Lisa Watts-Lawton, Second Grade
MaryJo Wieland, Second Grade
Jessa Woods, Second Grade

Eric Angel, Third Grade
Greg Gorman, Third Grade
Susan Lee, Third Grade
Cristina Metcalf, Third Grade
Ann Rose Santoro, Third Grade
Kevin Tougher, Third Grade
Victoria Peacock, Third Grade
Saffron VanGalder, Third Grade

Katrina Abdussalaam, Fourth Grade
Kelly Alsup, Fourth Grade
Patti Dieck, Fourth Grade
Mary Jones, Fourth Grade
Soojin Lu, Fourth Grade
Tricia Salerno, Fourth Grade
Gail Smith, Fourth Grade
Eric Welch, Fourth Grade
Sam Wertheim, Fourth Grade
Erin Wheeler, Fourth Grade

Leslie Arceneaux, Fifth Grade
Adam Baker, Fifth Grade
Janice Fan, Fifth Grade
Peggy Golden, Fifth Grade
Halle Kananak, Fifth Grade
Shauntina Kerrison, Fifth Grade
Pat Mohr, Fifth Grade
Chris Sarlo, Fifth Grade

## Additional Writers

Bill Davidson, Fluency Specialist
Robin Hecht, UDL Specialist
Simon Pfeil, Mathematician

## Document Management Team

Tam Le, Document Manager
Jennifer Merchan, Copy Editor

Table of Contents

# GRADE 2 • MODULE 2

Addition and Subtraction of Length Units

# Grade 2 • Module 2

# Addition and Subtraction of Length Units

## OVERVIEW

In this 12-day Grade 2 module, students engage in activities designed to deepen their conceptual understanding of measurement and to relate addition and subtraction to length. Their work in Module 2 is exclusively with metric units in order to support place value concepts. Customary units will be introduced in Module 7.

Topic A opens with students exploring concepts about the centimeter ruler. In the first lesson, they are guided to connect measurement with physical units as they find the total number of unit lengths by laying multiple copies of centimeter cubes (physical units) end-to-end along various objects. Through this, the students discover that to get an accurate measurement, there must not be any gaps or overlaps between consecutive length units.

Next, students measure by iterating with one physical unit, using the mark and advance technique. In the following lesson, students repeat the process by laying both multiple copies and a single cube along a centimeter ruler. This helps students create a mental benchmark for the centimeter. It also helps them realize that the distance between 0 and 1 on the ruler indicates the amount of space already covered. Hence 0, not 1, marks the beginning of the total length. Students use this understanding to create their own centimeter rulers using a centimeter cube and the mark and advance technique. Topic A ends with students using their unit rulers to measure lengths (**2.MD.1**), thereby connecting measurement with a ruler.

Students build skill in measuring using centimeter rulers and meter sticks in Topic B. They learn to see that a length unit is not a cube, or a portion of a ruler (which has width), but is a segment of a line. By measuring a variety of objects, students build a bank of known measurements or benchmark lengths, such as a doorknob being one meter from the floor, or the width of a finger being a centimeter. Then, students learn to estimate length using knowledge of previously measured objects and benchmarks. This enables students to internalize the mental rulers[1] of a centimeter or meter, which empowers them to mentally iterate units relevant to measuring a given length (**2.MD.3**). The knowledge and experience signal that students are determining which tool is appropriate to make certain measurements (**2.MD.1**).

In Topic C, students measure and compare to determine how much longer one object is than another (**2.MD.4**). They also measure objects twice using different length units, both standard and nonstandard, thereby developing their understanding of how the total measurement relates to the size of the length unit (**2.MD.2**). Repeated experience and explicit comparisons will help students recognize that the smaller the length unit, the larger the number of units, and the larger the length unit, the smaller the number of units.

The module culminates as students relate addition and subtraction to length. They apply their conceptual understanding to choose appropriate tools and strategies, such as the ruler as a number line, benchmarks for

---

[1] See the Progression Document "Geometric Measurement." page 14.

Module 2:    Addition and Subtraction of Length Units
Date:    6/26/13

ii

estimation, and tape diagrams for comparison, to solve word problems (**2.MD.5**, **2.MD.6**).  The problems progress from concrete (i.e., measuring objects and using the ruler as a number line to add and subtract) to abstract (i.e., representing lengths with tape diagrams to solve *start unknown* and two-step problems).

The end-of-module assessment follows Topic D.

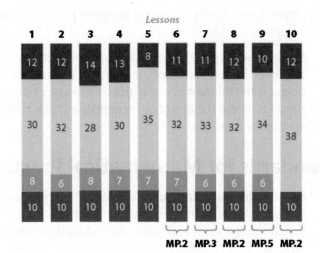

### Distribution of Instructional Minutes

This diagram represents a suggested distribution of instructional minutes based on the emphasis of particular lesson components in different lessons throughout the module.

■ **Fluency Practice**
□ **Concept Development**
■ **Application Problems**
■ **Student Debrief**

MP = Mathematical Practice

## Focus Grade Level Standards

### Measure and estimate lengths in standard units.[2]

**2.MD.1**   Measure the length of an object by selecting and using appropriate tools such as rulers, yardsticks, meter sticks, and measuring tapes.

**2.MD.2**   Measure the length of an object twice, using length units of different lengths for the two measurements; describe how the two measurements relate to the size of the unit chosen.

**2.MD.3**   Estimate lengths using units of inches, feet, centimeters, and meters.

**2.MD.4**   Measure to determine how much longer one object is than another, expressing the length difference in terms of a standard length unit.

### Relate addition and subtraction to length.

**2.MD.5**   Use addition and subtraction within 100 to solve word problems involving lengths that are given in the same units, e.g., by using drawings (such as drawings of rulers) and equations with a symbol for the unknown number to represent the problem.

---

[2] Focus is on metric measurement in preparation for place value in Module 3.  Customary measurement is addressed in Module 7.

**2.MD.6**    Represent whole numbers as lengths from 0 on a number line diagram with equally spaced points corresponding to the numbers 0, 1, 2, …, and represent whole-number sums and differences within 100 on a number line diagram.

## Foundational Standards

**1.MD.1**    Order three objects by length; compare the lengths of two objects indirectly by using a third object.

**1.MD.2**    Express the length of an object as a whole number of length units, by laying multiple copies of a shorter object (the length unit) end to end; understand that the length measurement of an object is the number of same-size length units that span it with no gaps or overlaps. *Limit to contexts where the object being measured is spanned by a whole number of length units with no gaps or overlaps.*

## Focus Standards for Mathematical Practice

**MP.2**    **Reason abstractly and quantitatively.** Students reason quantitatively when they measure and compare lengths. They reason abstractly when they use estimation strategies such as benchmarks and mental rulers, and when they relate number line diagrams to measurement models.

**MP.3**    **Construct viable arguments and critique the reasoning of others.** Students reason to solve word problems involving length measurement using tape diagrams and also analyze the reasonableness of the work of their peers.

**MP.5**    **Use appropriate tools strategically.** Students consider the object being measured and choose the appropriate measurement tool. They use the tool of the tape diagram to solve word problems.

**MP.6**    **Attend to precision.** Students accurately measure by laying physical units end-to-end with no gaps and when using a measurement tool. They correctly align the zero-point on a ruler as the beginning of the total length. They attend to precision when they verbally and in writing specify the length unit, when they use a ruler to measure or draw a straight line of a given length, and when they verify estimations by measuring.

Module 2:    Addition and Subtraction of Length Units
Date:        6/26/13

iv

# Overview of Module Topics and Lesson Objectives

| Standards | Topics and Objectives | | Days |
|---|---|---|---|
| **2.MD.1** | A | **Understand Concepts About the Ruler** | 3 |
| | | Lesson 1: Connect measurement with physical units by using multiple copies of the same physical unit to measure. | |
| | | Lesson 2: Use iteration with one physical unit to measure. | |
| | | Lesson 3: Apply concepts to create unit rulers and measure lengths using unit rulers. | |
| **2.MD.1**<br>**2.MD.3** | B | **Measure and Estimate Length Using Different Measurement Tools** | 2 |
| | | Lesson 4: Measure various objects using centimeter rulers and meter sticks. | |
| | | Lesson 5: Develop estimation strategies by applying prior knowledge of length and using mental benchmarks. | |
| **2.MD.1**<br>**2.MD.2**<br>**2.MD.4** | C | **Measure and Compare Lengths Using Different Length Units** | 2 |
| | | Lesson 6: Measure and compare lengths using centimeters and meters. | |
| | | Lesson 7: Measure and compare lengths using standard metric length units and non-standard lengths units; relate measurement to unit size. | |
| **2.MD.5**<br>**2.MD.6**<br>2.MD.1<br>2.MD.3<br>2.MD.4 | D | **Relate Addition and Subtraction to Length** | 3 |
| | | Lesson 8: Solve addition and subtraction word problems using the ruler as a number line. | |
| | | Lesson 9: Concrete to abstract: measure lengths of string using measurement tools; represent length with tape diagrams to represent and compare the lengths. | |
| | | Lesson 10: Apply conceptual understanding of measurement by solving two-step word problems | |
| | | End-of-Module Assessment:  Topics A–D  (assessment ½ day, return ½ day, remediation or further applications 1 day) | 2 |
| **Total Number of Instructional Days** | | | **12** |

# Terminology

## New or Recently Introduced Terms

Meter Strip

- Endpoint (where something ends, where measurement begins)
- Overlap (extend over, or cover partly)
- Ruler
- Centimeter (cm, unit of length measure)
- Meter
- Meter strip (pictured to the right)
- Meter stick
- Hash mark (the marks on a ruler or other measurement tool)
- Number line (a line marked at evenly spaced intervals)
- Estimate (an approximation of the value of a quantity or number)
- Benchmark (e.g., "round" numbers like multiples of 10)

## Familiar Terms and Symbols[3]

- Length
- Height
- Length Unit
- Combine
- Compare
- Difference
- Tape Diagram

# Suggested Tools and Representations

- Manipulatives that are 1 centimeter long (e.g., centimeter cubes)
- Centimeter ruler for each student
- Paper meter strips for each student
- Centimeter ruler, meter stick

---

[3] These are terms and symbols students have used or seen previously.

Module 2: Addition and Subtraction of Length Units
Date: 6/26/13

vi

# Scaffolds[4]

The scaffolds integrated into *A Story of Units* give alternatives for how students access information as well as express and demonstrate their learning. Strategically placed margin notes are provided within each lesson elaborating on the use of specific scaffolds at applicable times. They address many needs presented by English language learners, students with disabilities, students performing above grade level, and students performing below grade level. Many of the suggestions are organized by Universal Design for Learning (UDL) principles and are applicable to more than one population. To read more about the approach to differentiated instruction in *A Story of Units,* please refer to "How to Implement *A Story of Units*."

## Assessment Summary

| Type | Administered | Format | Standards Addressed |
|------|-------------|--------|---------------------|
| End-of-Module Assessment Task | After Topic D | Constructed response with rubric | 2.MD.1<br>2.MD.2<br>2.MD.3<br>2.MD.4<br>2.MD.5<br>2.MD.6 |

---

[4] Students with disabilities may require Braille, large print, audio, or special digital files. Please visit the website, www.p12.nysed.gov/specialed/aim, for specific information on how to obtain student materials that satisfy the National Instructional Materials Accessibility Standard (NIMAS) format.

# Mathematics Curriculum

## Topic A

# Understand Concepts About the Ruler

## 2.MD.1

| | | |
|---|---|---|
| **Focus Standard:** | 2.MD.1 | Measure the length of an object by selecting and using appropriate tools such as rulers, yardsticks, meter sticks, and measuring tapes. |
| **Instructional Days:** | 3 | |
| **Coherence** -Links from: | G1–M3 | Ordering and Comparing Length Measurements as Numbers |
| -Links to: | G3–M4 | Multiplication and Area |

Topic A begins with students exploring concepts about the ruler.  In Lesson 1, they relate length to physical units, by measuring various objects with multiple centimeter cubes.  Students create a mental benchmark for the centimeter.  In Lesson 2, they apply their knowledge of using centimeter cubes to measure by moving from repeated physical units to iteration of one physical unit.  This enables them to internalize their understanding of a length unit as the amount of space between one end of the cube to the other (or space between hash marks).  Thus, they begin moving from the concrete to the conceptual.  Finally, in Lesson 3, they apply knowledge of known measurements to create unit rulers using one centimeter cube.  This deepens the understanding of distance on a ruler and the ruler as a number line.

| A Teaching Sequence Towards Mastery of Understanding Concepts About the Ruler |
|---|
| **Objective 1:** Connect measurement with physical units by using multiple copies of the same physical unit to measure. <br> (Lesson 1) |
| **Objective 2:** Use iteration with one physical unit to measure. <br> (Lesson 2) |
| **Objective 3:** Apply concepts to create unit rulers and measure lengths using unit rules. <br> (Lesson 3) |

# Lesson 1

Objective:  Connect measurement with physical units by using multiple copies of the same physical unit to measure.

## Suggested Lesson Structure

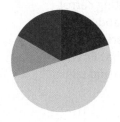

■ Fluency Practice          (12 minutes)
■ Application Problem        (8 minutes)
■ Concept Development        (30 minutes)
■ Student Debrief           (10 minutes)
  **Total Time**           **(60 minutes)**

## Fluency Practice  (12 minutes)

- Happy Counting 20–40 **2.NBT.2**          (2 minutes)
- Two More **2.OA.2**          (2 minutes)
- Before, Between, After **2.NBT.2**          (8 minutes)

Note:  These counting practices will help students prepare for counting centimeter cubes in the lesson.

### Happy Counting 20–40  (2 minutes)

T:   Let's do some Happy Counting!

T:   Let's count by ones, starting at 20.  Ready? (Teacher rhythmically points up until a change is desired. Show a closed hand then point down.  Continue, mixing it up.)

S:   20, 21, 22, 23 (stop) 22, 21, 20 (stop) 21, 22, 23, 24, 25 (stop) 24, 23, 22, 21, 20 (stop) 21, 22, 23, 24, 25, 26, 27, 28, 29, 30 (stop) 29, 28, 27, (stop) 28, 29, 30, 31, 32 (stop) 31, 30, 29, 28 (stop) 29, 30, 31, 32, 33, 34 (stop) 33, 32, 31, 30, 29 (stop) 30, 31, 32, 33, 34, 35, 36, 37, 38, 39, 40.

T:   Excellent!  Try it for 30 seconds with your partner starting at 28.  Partner A, you are the teacher today.

### Two More  (2 minutes)

T:   For every number I say, you will say what number is 2 more.  If I say 2, you would say 4.  Ready?  3.

S:   5.

Continue with possible sequences:  6, 8, 9, 18, 38, 58, 78, 79, 19, 29, 39.

Lesson 1:        Connect measurement with physical units by using multiple copies
                 of the same physical unit to measure.
Date:            6/26/13

2.A.2

## Sprint: Before, Between, After (8 minutes)

Materials: (S) Before, Between, After Sprint

## Application Problem (8 minutes)

At the lunch table, Mariana, Billy, and Emma are eating carrot sticks. Billy's carrot sticks are longer than Emma's, and Mariana's carrot sticks are longer than Billy's. If Mariana's carrot sticks are 12 centimeters long, is it possible that Emma's carrot sticks are 7 centimeters long? Draw a picture and use words to explain your thinking.

What is one possible length for Billy's carrot sticks?

**NOTES ON MULTIPLE MEANS OF ENGAGEMENT:**

Some students may struggle to comprehend the transitive property. Divide the problem into small, workable chunks, so students can read and draw one step at a time. For example:

- T: Billy's carrot sticks are longer than Emma's.

- S: (Draws 2 carrot sticks and labels them.)

- T: Mariana's carrot sticks are longer than Billy's.

- S: (Draws a third carrot stick and labels it, etc.)

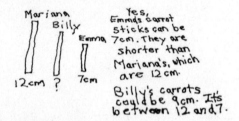

Note: In Grade 1, students spend time comparing the lengths of two objects indirectly by using a third object (1.MD.1). In this problem, students practice working with the transitive property using comparative language. While the teacher circulates and provides support, students use personal boards to draw a picture and compare with a partner before participating in a whole-class discussion. The teacher may wish to segue into today's lesson by asking students if they could measure the carrot sticks with a small paper clip.

## Concept Development (30 minutes)

Materials: (T) 2–3 crayons with varying lengths (S) Baggie with 30 or more centimeter cubes for each pair of students, baggie of used crayons for each pair of students, 2 pencil boxes, 1 fork

- T: (Call students to sit in a circle on the carpet.) I was looking at my pencil box this morning, and I was very curious about how long it might be. I also have this handful of **centimeter** cubes and I thought I might be able to measure the length of my pencil box with these cubes. Does anyone have an idea about how I might do that?

- S: You could put the cubes in a line along the pencil box and count how many!

- T: Does anyone want to **estimate** how many centimeter cubes long it will be?

- S: (Students make estimates.)

Lesson 1: Connect measurement with physical units by using multiple copies of the same physical unit to measure.

Date: 6/26/13

2.A.3

T:   Let's see how many centimeter cubes we can line up along the length of the pencil box.  (Teacher lays cubes along the length of the first pencil box with random spaces in between each cube.)T: OK. Should I go ahead and count my cubes now?

S:   No!

T:   Why not?

S:   You need to put the cubes right next to each other.

T:   Aha!  Come show me how you would place the cubes to measure this second pencil box.  (Student volunteer lays the cubes along the length of the second pencil box with no space in between each cube.  Demonstrate in center of circle so students can see alignment.)

**NOTES ON MULTIPLE MEANS OF REPRESENTATION:**

Post conversation starters during *think–pair–share* while measuring with cubes:

- Your solution is different from mine because . . .
- Your error was . . .
- My strategy was to . . .

These sentence starters will also be useful in the Student Debrief portion of the lesson.

T:   Let's count the cubes my way and your way.  (Teacher and students count the cubes chorally, teacher writes both measurements on the board.)

T:   Turn to your neighbor and tell them why there is a difference between my number of cubes and your number of cubes.

S:   You had fewer cubes because there were some empty spaces.  → If you push all the cubes together you have a lot of extra space not measured.

T:   Now you will work with a partner to measure a set of used crayons.  Each crayon will be a different length and some may not be an exact measurement.

T:   (Hold up a crayon with a measurement that will be rounded up.)

T:   Notice that this crayon is almost 8 centimeter cubes long.  It is more than 7.5 cubes but not quite 8.  I can say this crayon is about 8 centimeter cubes long.

T:   (Hold up a crayon with a measurement that will be rounded down.)

T:   Notice that this crayon is close to 6 centimeter cubes long.  It is just a little bit longer than 6 cubes and not half way to 7 cubes.  How long would you say this crayon is?

S:   About 6 centimeter cubes.

T:   Now you will work with a partner to measure a set of used crayons.  As you measure, be sure to use the word *about* to describe a measurement that is not exact.  Turn to your neighbor and estimate how many centimeter cubes you think you will need for each crayon in the baggie.  (Students share estimates with their partner and then begin measuring their crayons.)  (Alternative items to measure are scissors, each other's pencils, erasers, etc.)

T:   Let's practice some more measuring on our activity sheet.

| | Lesson 1: | Connect measurement with physical units by using multiple copies of the same physical unit to measure. | 2.A.4 |
| | Date: | 6/26/13 | |

## Problem Set  (10 minutes)

Students should do their personal best to complete the Problem Set within the allotted 10 minutes.  Some problems do not specify a method for solving.  This is an intentional reduction of scaffolding that invokes MP.5, Use Appropriate Tools Strategically.  Students should solve these problems using the RDW approach used for Application Problems.

For some classes, it may be appropriate to modify the assignment by specifying which problems students should work on first. With this option, let the careful sequencing of the problem set guide your selections so that problems continue to be scaffolded.  Balance word problems with other problem types to ensure a range of practice.  Assign incomplete problems for homework or at another time during the day.

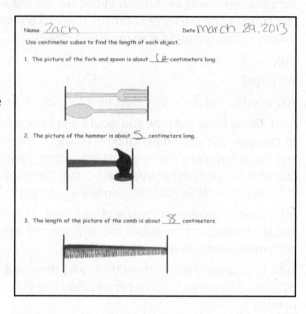

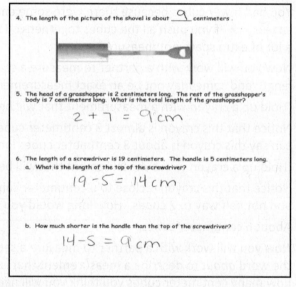

## Student Debrief  (10 minutes)

Lesson Objective:  Connect measurement with physical units by using multiple copies of the same physical unit to measure.

The Student Debrief is intended to invite reflection and active processing of the total lesson experience.

Invite students to review their solutions for the Problem Set.  They should check work by comparing answers with a partner before going over answers as a class.  Look for misconceptions or misunderstandings that can be addressed in the Debrief.  Guide students in a conversation to debrief the Problem Set and process the lesson.  You may choose to use any combination of the questions below to lead the discussion.

MP.3

- Turn to your partner and compare your answers to Problems 1–4.  What did you need to be sure to do?

- Did anyone find when sharing their work that they had a different measurement than their neighbor?  Why do you think that happened?  (Students will share that they may have not lined up the object with the edge of the first **centimeter** cube, or that they left spaces between cubes.  This is an excellent opportunity to discuss **endpoint** and **overlap**.)

- How did your drawings help you to answer Problems 5 and 6?

COMMON CORE

Lesson 1:

Date:

Connect measurement with physical units by using multiple copies of the same physical unit to measure.
6/26/13

2.A.5

- What new (or significant) vocabulary did we use today to talk about measurement? (*Length, estimate, longer.*)
- What did you learn about how to measure with centimeter cubes? Could you have measured with a pocketful of coins?

## Exit Ticket (3 minutes)

After the Student Debrief, instruct students to complete the Exit Ticket. A review of their work will help you assess the students' understanding of the concepts that were presented in the lesson today and plan more effectively for future lessons. You may read the questions aloud to the students.

Note: Discuss Homework Problems 3 and 4 during the next day's lesson.

Lesson 1:   Connect measurement with physical units by using multiple copies
of the same physical unit to measure.

Date:   6/26/13

2.A.6

**A**

# Correct _____

Add or subtract.

| | | | | | | |
|---|---|---|---|---|---|---|
| 1 | 1, 2, ___ | | 23 | 99, ___, 101 | |
| 2 | 11, 12, ___ | | 24 | 19, 20, ___ | |
| 3 | 21, 22, ___ | | 25 | 119, 120, ___ | |
| 4 | 71, 72, ___ | | 26 | 35, ___, 37 | |
| 5 | 3, 4, ___ | | 27 | 135, ___, 137 | |
| 6 | 3, ___, 5 | | 28 | ___, 24, 25 | |
| 7 | 13, ___, 15 | | 29 | ___, 124, 125 | |
| 8 | 23, ___, 25 | | 30 | 142, 143, ___ | |
| 9 | 83, ___, 85 | | 31 | 138, ___, 140 | |
| 10 | 7, 8, ___ | | 32 | ___, 149, 150 | |
| 11 | 7, ___, 9 | | 33 | 148, ___, 150 | |
| 12 | ___, 8, 9 | | 34 | ___, 149, 150 | |
| 13 | ___, 18, 19 | | 35 | ___, 163, 164 | |
| 14 | ___, 28, 29 | | 36 | 187, ___, 189 | |
| 15 | ___, 58, 59 | | 37 | ___, 170, 171 | |
| 16 | 12, 13, ___ | | 38 | 178, 179, ___ | |
| 17 | 45, 46, ___ | | 39 | 192, ___, 194 | |
| 18 | 12, ___, 14 | | 40 | ___, 190, 191 | |
| 19 | 36, ___, 38 | | 41 | 197, ___, 199 | |
| 20 | ___, 19, 20 | | 42 | 168, 169, ___ | |
| 21 | ___, 89, 90 | | 43 | 199, ___, 201 | |
| 22 | 98, 99, ___ | | 44 | ___, 160, 161 | |

© Bill Davidson
bdavidson40@gmail.com

Lesson 1:     Connect measurement with physical units by using multiple copies
of the same physical unit to measure.
Date:     6/26/13

2.A.7

**B**

Improvement _____    # Correct _____

Add or subtract.

| # | Problem | | # | Problem | |
|---|---------|---|---|---------|---|
| 1 | 0, 1, ___ | | 23 | 99, ___, 101 | |
| 2 | 10, 11, ___ | | 24 | 29, 30, ___ | |
| 3 | 20, 21, ___ | | 25 | 129, 130, ___ | |
| 4 | 70, 71, ___ | | 26 | 34, ___, 36 | |
| 5 | 2, 3, ___ | | 27 | 134, ___, 136 | |
| 6 | 2, ___, 4 | | 28 | ___, 23, 24 | |
| 7 | 12, ___, 14 | | 29 | ___, 123, 124 | |
| 8 | 22, ___, 24 | | 30 | 141, 142, ___ | |
| 9 | 82, ___, 84 | | 31 | 128, ___, 130 | |
| 10 | 6, 7, ___ | | 32 | ___, 149, 150 | |
| 11 | 6, ___, 8 | | 33 | 148, ___, 150 | |
| 12 | ___, 7, 8 | | 34 | ___, 149, 150 | |
| 13 | ___, 17, 18 | | 35 | ___, 173, 174 | |
| 14 | ___, 27, 28 | | 36 | 167, ___, 169 | |
| 15 | ___, 57, 58 | | 37 | ___, 160, 161 | |
| 16 | 11, 12, ___ | | 38 | 188, 189, ___ | |
| 17 | 44, 45, ___ | | 39 | 193, ___, 195 | |
| 18 | 11, ___, 13 | | 40 | ___, 170, 171 | |
| 19 | 35, ___, 37 | | 41 | 196, ___, 198 | |
| 20 | ___, 19, 20 | | 42 | 178, 179, ___ | |
| 21 | ___, 79, 80 | | 43 | 199, ___, 201 | |
| 22 | 98, 99, ___ | | 44 | ___, 180, 181 | |

© Bill Davidson
bdavidson40@gmail.com

**Lesson 1:**    Connect measurement with physical units by using multiple copies
of the same physical unit to measure.

**Date:**    6/26/13

2.A.8

Name _____ Date _____

Use centimeter cubes to find the length of each object.

1.  The picture of the fork and spoon is about _____ centimeters long.

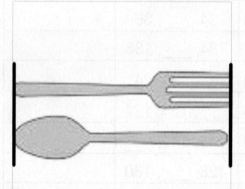

2.  The picture of the hammer is about _____ centimeters long.

3.  The length of the picture of the comb is about _____ centimeters.

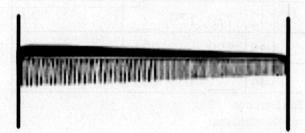

**COMMON CORE** | Lesson 1: | Connect measurement with physical units by using multiple copies of the same physical unit to measure.
Date: | 6/26/13

2.A.9

4. The length of the picture of the shovel is about _____ centimeters .

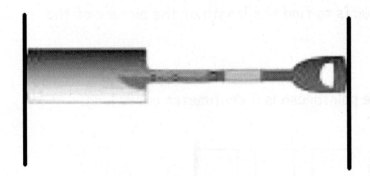

5. The head of a grasshopper is 2 centimeters long.  The rest of the grasshopper's body is 7 centimeters long.  What is the total length of the grasshopper?

6. The length of a screwdriver is 19 centimeters.  The handle is 5 centimeters long.

   a. What is the length of the top of the screwdriver?

   b. How much shorter is the handle than the top of the screwdriver?

**COMMON CORE** | **Lesson 1:** Connect measurement with physical units by using multiple copies of the same physical unit to measure. 2.A.10

**Date:** 6/26/13

Name _____     Date _____

1.  Sara lined up her centimeter cubes to find the length of the picture of the paintbrush.

    Sarah thinks the picture of the paintbrush is 5 centimeter cubes long.

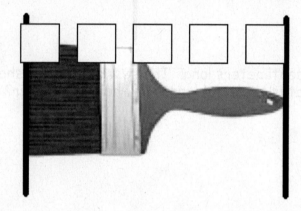

    Is her answer correct?  Explain why or why not.

    _____

    _____

**COMMON CORE**™      Lesson 1:     Connect measurement with physical units by using multiple copies
                            of the same physical unit to measure.                                              **2.A.11**
                    Date:        6/26/13

Name _____ Date _____

Count each centimeter cube to find the length of each object.

1.

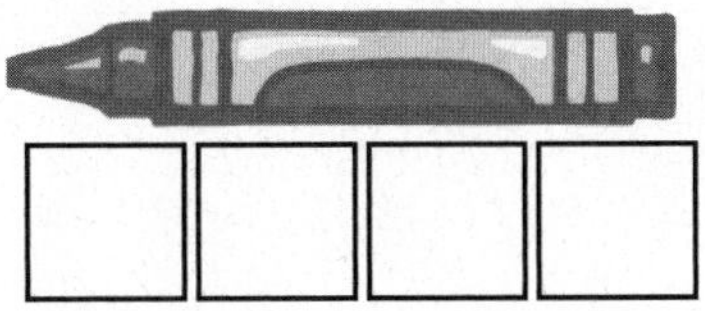

The crayon is _____ centimeter cubes long.

2.

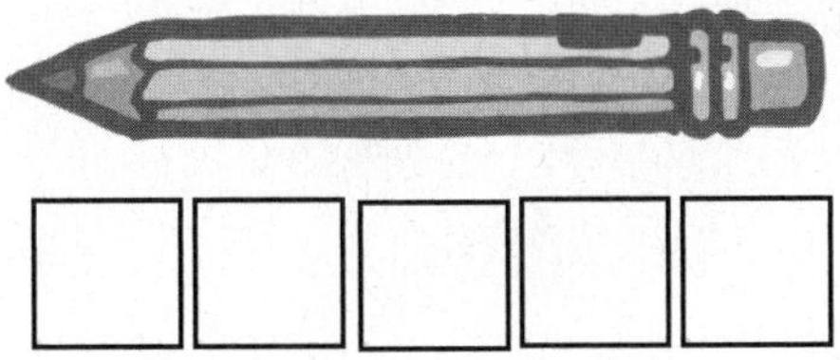

The pencil is _____ centimeter cubes long.

3.

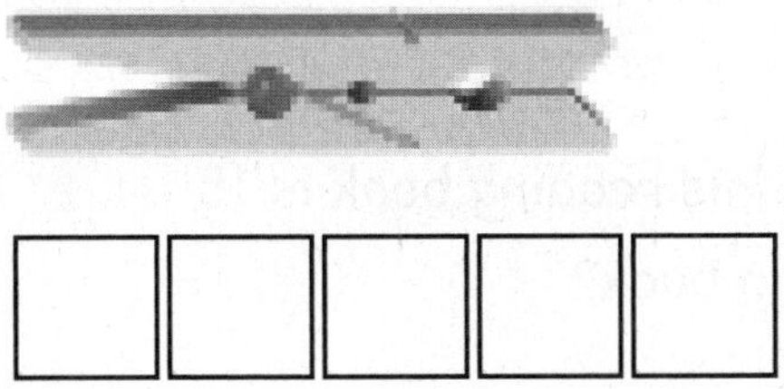

The clothespin is _____ centimeters.

4.

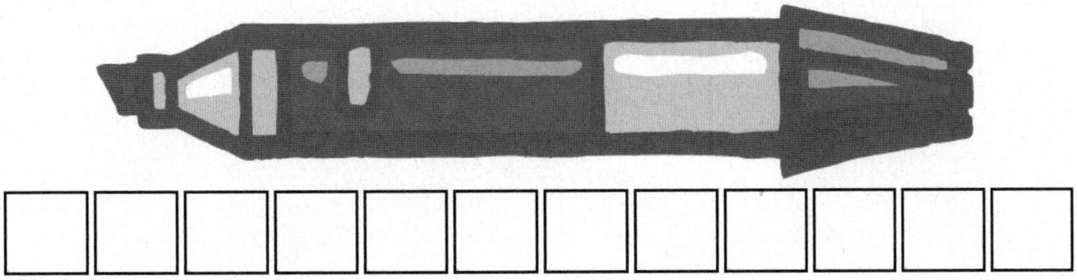

The length of the marker is _____ centimeters.

**COMMON CORE**™ | Lesson 1: | Connect measurement with physical units by using multiple copies of the same physical unit to measure. | 2.A.12

Date: 6/26/13

5.  Richard has 43 centimeter cubes.  Henry has 36 centimeter cubes.  What is the length of their cubes altogether?

6.  The length of Marisa's loaf of bread is 56 centimeters.  She cut off of 32 centimeters of bread.  What is the length of what she has left?

7.  The length of Jimmy's math book is 19 centimeter cubes.  His reading book is 15 centimeter cubes longer.  What is the length of his reading book?

**COMMON CORE**   Lesson 1:   Connect measurement with physical units by using multiple copies                2.A.13
                          of the same physical unit to measure.
                 Date:     6/26/13

© 2013 Common Core, Inc. All rights reserved. commoncore.org

# Lesson 2

Objective: Use iteration with one physical unit to measure.

## Suggested Lesson Structure

■ Fluency Practice      (12 minutes)
■ Application Problems   (6 minutes)
■ Concept Development  (32 minutes)
■ Student Debrief       (10 minutes)
  **Total Time**        **(60 minutes)**

## Fluency Practice (12 minutes)

- Say Ten Counting **2.NBT.1**           (2 minutes)
- Say Ten Counting to the Next Ten **2.NBT.1**   (4 minutes)
- Make Ten to Add **2.OA.2**          (6 minutes)

Note: This fluency reviews skills taught in Module 1 and will reinforce using place value concepts to add.

## Say Ten Counting (2 minutes)

T: Let's count the *say ten way*. When I say 52, you say 5 tens 2. Ready? 67.
S: 6 tens 7.
T: 98.
S: 9 tens 8.
T: 100.
S: 10 tens.
T: 113.
S: 11 tens 3.

Continue with possible sequence: 103, 123, 127, 137, 132, 142, 143, 163, 168, 188, 198, 200.

## Say Ten Counting to the Next Ten (4 minutes)

T: Let's add to make the next ten the say ten way. I say 5 tens 2, you say 5 tens 2 + 8 = 6 tens. Ready? 6 tens 7.
S: 6 tens 7 + 3 = 7 tens.
T: 5 tens 1.
S: 5 tens 1 + 9 = 6 tens.

Lesson 2:   Use iteration with one physical unit to measure.
Date:     6/26/13

2.A.14

T:   7 tens 8.

S:   7 tens 8 + 2 = 8 tens.

Continue with possible sequence:  8 tens 4, 8 tens 5, 8 tens 9, 9 tens 6, 9 tens 3, and 9 tens 9.

## Make Ten to Add  (6 minutes)

T:   Let's make 10 to add.  If I say 9 + 2, you say 9 + 2 = 10 + 1.  Ready?  9 + 3.

S:   9 + 3 = 10 + 2.

T:   Answer?

S:   12.

T:   9 + 5.

S:   9 + 5 = 10 + 4.

T:   Answer?

S:   14.

Continue with possible sequence:  9 + 7, 9 + 6, 9 + 8, 8 + 3, 8 + 5, 7 + 4, and 7 + 6.

T:   On your personal board, write at least 3 other similar examples.


## Application Problem  (6 minutes)

Kaela is making 4 bracelets, and she wants them to be the same length.  She found a jar of square Lego pieces that are all about the size of her thumbnail.  How can she use these Lego pieces to measure the length of the bracelets?  Draw a picture and use words to explain your thinking.

What could Kaela do if she only had one Lego piece?

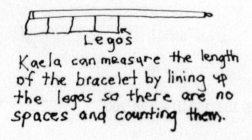

Kaela can measure the length of the bracelet by lining up the legos so there are no spaces and counting them.

**NOTES ON ROUNDING MEASUREMENTS:**

When students are measuring with centimeter cubes, teach them to round up or down depending on the situation.  If the length past the exact centimeter mark is half a centimeter, students will round up, if it is less, students will round down.  Teach students to use words such as *about*, *approximately*, *exactly*, and *around* to describe their measurements.

Note:  Today's problem reviews the concept of measuring using multiple copies of the same physical unit.  The second question sets the stage for today's objective, using iteration with one physical unit to measure.  Students can brainstorm their ideas with a partner and create a shared picture and written statement to illustrate their understanding.  Then, students return to the carpet with their completed work and explain their reasoning orally.

| | Lesson 2: | Use iteration with one physical unit to measure. |
|---|---|---|
| | Date: | 6/26/13 |

2.A.15

## Concept Development (32 minutes)

Materials: (T/S) Baggie with 1 centimeter cube, 1 long paper clip, 3 linking cubes (joined), 1 crayon, dry erase marker, 1 post-it note, 1 index card, a pencil, and paper

T: (Call students to the carpet.) Yesterday we measured a pencil box together using many centimeter cubes. Today we will measure some other objects, but this time we will only use one centimeter cube.

T: Think back to the two different ways we measured the pencil boxes yesterday. Ask your partner, what was I doing wrong yesterday?

S: You left spaces between the cubes. → You were supposed to put the cubes right next to each other.

T: How could we measure with one cube? Turn to your neighbor and tell them what you think.

S: You could put the cube down and then put your finger down to show where it ends. → You could mark the end with a pencil.

T: (Teacher models measuring the paper clip with one centimeter cube using the *mark and move forward* technique. Use a document camera or an overhead for students to be able to see. If such technology is unavailable, use a thousands block base-ten cube to measure a line drawn on the board to show students the mark and move forward technique.)

T: Watch my measurement strategy. I make a mark where the cube ends. (Do so.) Then I move my cube forward so that the mark is right at the beginning of the cube. (Do so.) I mark where the cube ends again. Now talk to your partner about what I'll do next.

S: Move the cube forward so the new mark is at the beginning of the cube!

T: What did you notice about how I measured with my centimeter cube?

S: You didn't leave any space between your pencil mark and the centimeter cube. → Your pencil line is very tiny. → You put the edge of the cube down right on the line.

T: What do you notice about the spaces I've made? Talk with your partner.

S: They're all the same length.

T: When I measured my paperclip the length was just a little less than 3 cm. I can say my paperclip is *about* 3 cm because it is very close. If the measurement is halfway or more to the next centimeter we round up. Otherwise we round down.

NOTES ON MULTIPLE MEANS OF ACTION AND EXPRESSION:

Get moving! Demonstrate the iteration strategy by calling a student forward to measure the chalkboard with his/her body, placing marks on either side of the student's shoulders and continuing to move forward along the length of the chalkboard.

T: Now it's your turn to measure. Open your bag and take out the paper clip and the centimeter cube.

T: Put the paper clip on your paper. Now put your centimeter cube down alongside the paper clip. Make sure your centimeter cube is exactly even with the start of your paper clip.

Lesson 2:    Use iteration with one physical unit to measure.
Date:    6/26/13

2.A.16

S:  (Students begin measuring as the teacher walks them through the mark and move forward strategy.)

T:  How many centimeters long is the paper clip?  Thumbs up when you have your answer.

S:  4 centimeters!

T:  Let's measure the crayon this time.  Give me a thumbs-up when you know the length of the crayon.  (Discuss answer with class.)

**MP.6**

Next, have the students measure the linking cube stick.  Send students to their seats to measure the remaining items in their bags. Keep students who need extra support on the carpet to guide them.

**NOTES ON MULTIPLE MEANS OF REPRESENTATION:**

For Problem 5 on the Problem Set, clarify and make connections to important math concepts:  repeating equal units, mark and move forward strategy.

Model written response starters, such as, "Elijah's answer will be incorrect, because …"

## Problem Set  (10 minutes)

Students should do their personal best to complete the Problem Set within the allotted 10 minutes.  For some classes, it may be appropriate to modify the assignment by specifying which problems they work on first.  Some problems do not specify a method for solving.  Students solve these problems using the RDW approach used for Application Problems.

## Student Debrief  (10 minutes)

**Lesson Objective**:  Use iteration with one physical unit to measure.

The Student Debrief is intended to invite reflection and active processing of the total lesson experience.

Invite students to review their solutions for the Problem Set.  They should check work by comparing answers with a partner before going over answers as a class.  Look for misconceptions or misunderstandings that can be addressed in the Debrief.  Guide students in a conversation to debrief the Problem Set and process the lesson.  You may choose to use any combination of the questions below to lead the discussion

- Compare your answers to Problems 1–3 with a partner?  What did you do to measure accurately?

- What were your thoughts about Elijah's estimation in Problem 5?  (Students share answers.  Elicit and reinforce the repetition of equal units being necessary to measure.)

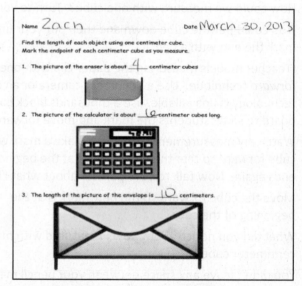

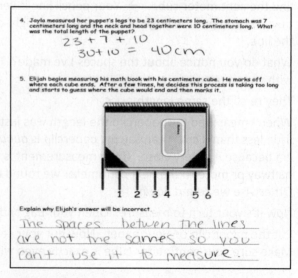

**COMMON CORE**

Lesson 2:  Use iteration with one physical unit to measure.
Date:  6/26/13

2.A.17

- Turn and talk: Why do you think I called today's strategy for measuring the mark and move forward strategy?

- Which method for measuring do you think is better, easier, or quicker? Measuring with multiple cubes or measuring with just one cube? Why?

- During our lesson, we measured three linking cubes with centimeter cubes. Could we use a linking cube to measure instead of a centimeter cube? Let's measure the picture of Elijah's notebook with one linking cube. What do you notice?

## Exit Ticket (3 minutes)

After the Student Debrief, instruct students to complete the Exit Ticket. A review of their work will help you assess the students' understanding of the concepts that were presented in the lesson today and plan more effectively for future lessons. You may read the questions aloud to the students.

Name _____ Date _____

Find the length of each object using one centimeter cube. Mark the endpoint of each centimeter cube as you measure.

1. The picture of the eraser is about _____ centimeter cubes

2. The picture of the calculator is about _____ centimeter cubes long.

3. The length of the picture of the envelope is _____ centimeters.

**COMMON CORE**

Lesson 2:    Use iteration with one physical unit to measure.
Date:     6/26/13

2.A.19

4. Jayla measured her puppet's legs to be 23 centimeters long. The stomach was 7 centimeters long and the neck and head together were 10 centimeters long. What was the total length of the puppet?

5. Elijah begins measuring his math book with his centimeter cube. He marks off where each cube ends. After a few times, he decides this process is taking too long and starts to guess where the cube would end and then marks it.

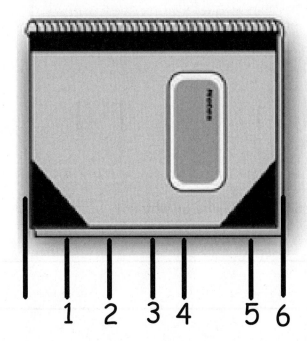

1   2   3 4     5 6

Explain why Elijah's answer will be incorrect.

_____

_____

_____

Name _____ Date _____

1. Matt measured his index card using a centimeter cube. He marked the endpoint of the cube as he measured. He thinks the index card is 10 centimeters long.

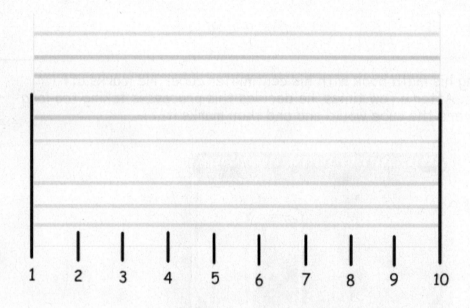

a. Is Matt's work correct? Explain why or why not.

_____

_____

_____

b. If you were Matt's teacher what would you tell him?

_____

_____

_____

Name _____     Date _____

Use the centimeter cube on the next page to measure the length of each object.
Mark the endpoint of the cube as you measure.

1.  The picture of the glue is about _____ centimeters long.

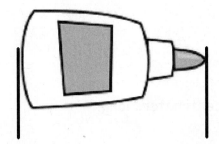

2.  The picture of the lollypop is about _____ centimeters long.

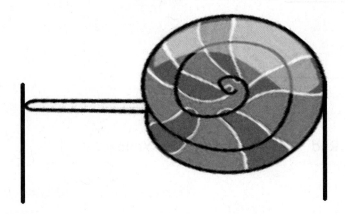

3.  The picture of the scissors is about _____ centimeters long.

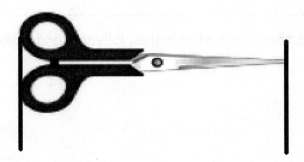

**COMMON CORE**     Lesson 2:     Use iteration with one physical unit to measure.
                    Date:        6/26/13

2.A.22

Red Ribbon

Blue Ribbon

Yellow Ribbon

a. How long is the red ribbon? _____ centimeters long.

b. How long is the blue ribbon? _____ centimeters long.

c. How long is the yellow ribbon? _____ centimeters long.

d. Which ribbon is the longest?     Red          Blue          Yellow

e. Which ribbon is the shortest?  Red          Blue          Yellow

f. The total length of all the ribbons is _____ centimeters.

-------------------------------------------------------------------------------

Cut out this centimeter cube to measure the length of the glue, lollypop, and scissors.

# Lesson 3

Objective: Apply concepts to create unit rulers and measure lengths using unit rulers.

## Suggested Lesson Structure

■ Fluency Practice          (14 minutes)
■ Application Problems    (8 minutes)
□ Concept Development   (28 minutes)
■ Student Debrief        (10 minutes)
   **Total Time**            **(60 minutes)**

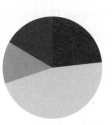

## Fluency Practice (14 minutes)

▪ Happy Counting 40–60 **2.NBT.2**                         (2 minutes)
▪ Making 10 by Identifying the Missing Part **2.OA.2**     (3 minutes)
▪ Making 10 **2.OA.2**                                     (9 minutes)

### Happy Counting 40–60 (2 minutes)

T:   Let's do some Happy Counting!

T:   Let's count by ones, starting at 40. Ready? (Teacher rhythmically points up until a change is desired. Show a closed hand then point down. Continue, mixing it up.)

S:   40, 41, 42, 43, (stop), 42, 41, 40, (stop), 41, 42, 43, 44, 45 (stop) 44, 43, 42, 41, 40 (stop) 41, 42, 43, 44, 45, 46, 47, 48, 49, 50 (stop) 49, 48, 47, (stop) 48, 49, 50, 51, 52 (stop) 51, 50, 49, 48 (stop) 49, 50, 51, 52, 53, 54 (stop) 53, 52, 51, 50, 49 (stop) 50, 51, 52, 53, 54, 55, 56, 57, 58, 59, 60.

T:   Excellent! Try it for 30 seconds with your partner starting at 48. Partner B, you are the teacher today.

### Make 10 by Identifying the Missing Part (3 minutes)

Materials: (S) Personal white boards

T:   If I say 9, you say 1 because 9 and 1 make 10.

T:   Wait for the signal, 15. (Signal with a snap.)

S:   5.

T:   (Continue with possible sequence: 18, 12, 29, 21, etc.)

Lesson 3:     Apply concepts to create unit rulers, measure lengths using unit rulers.
Date:     6/26/13

**2.A.24**

T:  This time I'll say a number and you write the addition sentence to make ten on your personal white board.

T:  19. Get ready. Show me your board.

S:  (Students write 19 + 1 = 20.)

T:  Get ready. Show me your board.

T:  (Continue with possible sequence: 18, 12, 25, 29, and 45)

T:  Turn and tell your partner what pattern you noticed that helped you solve the problems.

T:  Turn and tell your partner your strategy for finding the missing part.

## Sprint:  Making 10  (9 minutes)

Materials:  (S) Making Ten Sprint

## Application Problem  (8 minutes)

Jared's parents buy him a new bed, but they are not sure if it is short enough to fit against his bedroom wall. Jared only has his dad's construction boot and a popsicle stick as measurement tools. Which measurement strategy would you suggest to Jared? (Students turn and talk to their partner and discuss the mark and move forward strategy.)

Can Jared figure out if the new bed will fit in his bedroom? How do you know? Use numbers, pictures, or words to explain your thinking.

Extension:  Which tool would you use to measure, the popsicle stick or the construction boot? Why?

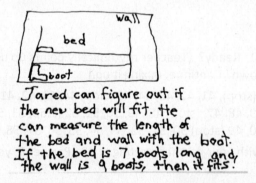

Note:  The first portion of this problem reviews using iteration with one physical unit to measure and asks students to recall the mark and move forward strategy. The second portion asks the student to make a comparison between the length of Jared's bed and the length of his bedroom wall and decide if the bed is short enough to fit. During the second portion, students use personal white boards to draw a picture, adding numbers and words to support their conclusions. The extension portion is designed for accelerated learners, as this measurement concept of inverse relationship will not be addressed until Lesson 7. When all students have had a reasonable amount of time to work, they trade work with a partner. The teacher circulates and chooses a few students to share their partner's work aloud.

 Lesson 3:  Apply concepts to create unit rulers, measure lengths using unit rulers.
Date:  6/26/13

2.A.25

## Concept Development  (28 minutes)

Materials:  (S) 1 30-cm long x 5-cm wide strip of tag board or sentence strips, 1 centimeter cube, and 1 index
card or post-it note per student

T: Yesterday we used 1 centimeter cube to measure the
length of different objects.  Today we're going to
create a tool that will help us measure centimeters in a
more efficient way.

**NOTES TO**
**THE TEACHER:**

T:   Let's make a centimeter **ruler**!  Watch how I use my
centimeter cube to measure and mark centimeters
onto the tag board.

In order for students to create an
accurate ruler, the hash marks have to
be precise.  Show students they can
make their marks precise by placing the
centimeter cube directly below the tag
board and making a line where the
cube ends.  By doing this, students
avoid adding an incremental amount to
each length unit.

T:   (Teacher models placing the cube and using the mark
and move forward strategy to show 4 cm.)  What did
you notice about how I marked my tag board?

S:   You did what we did yesterday.  → You didn't leave
any space between the cube and your pencil mark.  →
You made all the spaces (intervals) the same size.  →
You called it the mark and move forward strategy.

T:   Now take out your tag board, centimeter cube, and pencil.  Let's do a few centimeters together.
(Turn tag board over and guide students to make their first 3 cm along with you.)

Support students who need assistance and allow those who
show mastery to complete their rulers independently.  As
students complete their rulers direct them to explore measuring
items around the room.

**NOTES ON**
**MULTIPLE MEANS**
**OF REPRESENTATION:**

After all students have completed their rulers invite them to the
carpet with their rulers, centimeter cubes, index cards and
pencils.

Glue a toothpick or wikki stix to
represent each of the hash marks for
blind or visually impaired students,
enabling them to feel the length units
on their ruler.

T:   You have all completed a centimeter ruler.  Now I
would like to explore how we can use this tool.  Let's
take a look at some of the objects students measured
around the room.  I see that someone measured a
math book.  Let's take a look at how we might do that.

T:   Turn to your neighbor and tell him how you would use your centimeter ruler to measure the length
of your math book.

S:   You can put the ruler next to the book and count how many lines.  → Line up the ruler with the edge
of the math book.  Count how many lines there are.

T:   (Line ruler up with the edge of the math book.  Count the **hash marks** chorally with the students.)  I
am noticing there is a lot of room for mistakes here with so much counting.  Does anyone have an
idea about how I could make this easier the next time I use my ruler?

S:   You can mark the lines with numbers!

| Lesson 3: | Apply concepts to create unit rulers, measure lengths using unit rulers. |
|---|---|
| Date: | 6/26/13 |

**2.A.26**

T:   It is a wise idea to mark the lines with numbers. I can keep count more easily and also next time I won't have to count again. (Model marking the first two centimeters.)

T:   Notice I am making my numbers small so they fit right on top of the hash marks. Now it's your turn.

(As students show mastery of marking their rulers with numbers, allow them to complete the numbers for all 30 hash marks.)

T:   Now that we have our rulers complete, let's practice using them together. Take out your index cards. Where should I place my ruler to measure the long side of the index card? Turn to your neighbor and tell them what you think.

(Guide students through measuring their index card and at least two more objects such as their pencil and pencil box. As they show mastery send them to their seats to complete the activity worksheet. If students need more practice, provide them with more opportunity, such as measuring their pencil.)

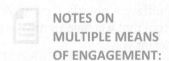

**NOTES ON MULTIPLE MEANS OF ENGAGEMENT:**

Assign students a *measurement discovery buddy* to clarify directions and/or processes. Buddies compare answers to check their work.

## Problem Set  (7 minutes)

Students should do their personal best to complete the Problem Set within the allotted 7 minutes. For some classes, it may be appropriate to modify the assignment by specifying which problems they work on first. Some problems do not specify a method for solving. Students solve these problems using the RDW approach used for Application Problems.

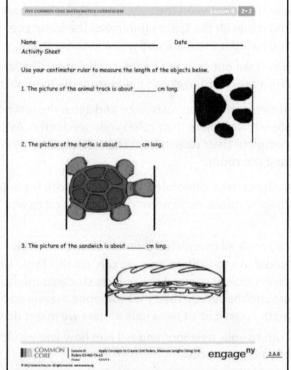

## Student Debrief  (10 minutes)

**Lesson Objective:**  Apply concepts to create unit rulers, measure lengths using unit rulers.

The Student Debrief is intended to invite reflection and active processing of the total lesson experience.

Invite students to review their solutions for the Problem Set. They should check work by comparing answers with a partner before going over answers as a class. Look for misconceptions or misunderstandings that can be addressed in the Debrief. Guide students in a conversation to debrief the Problem Set and process the lesson.

You may choose to use any combination of the questions below to lead the discussion.

- Turn to your partner and compare your measurements on Problems 1–3. What did you do to measure accurately with your centimeter **ruler**?

Lesson 3:    Apply concepts to create unit rulers, measure lengths using unit rulers.
Date:        6/26/13

2.A.27

- Tell your partner about how you made your ruler. What steps did you take to make it an accurate tool for measurement?

- What was different about using the mark and move forward strategy from using the ruler? Why is using the ruler more efficient than counting **hash marks**?

- Let's look at Problem 4(c) on the Problem Set. How could we use similar words to fit the situation in our application problem (How much shorter is the length of Jared's bed than the length of his bedroom wall?). What strategy would you suggest to compare the two lengths?

- What are some objects that are longer than our centimeter rulers? How can we measure objects that are longer than our rulers?

## Exit Ticket (3 minutes)

After the Student Debrief, instruct students to complete the Exit Ticket. A review of their work will help you assess the students' understanding of the concepts that were presented in the lesson today and plan more effectively for future lessons. You may read the questions aloud to the students.

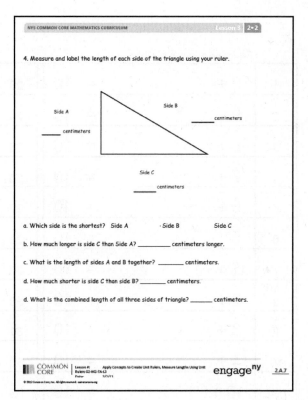

COMMON CORE™

Lesson 3: Apply concepts to create unit rulers, measure lengths using unit rulers.

Date: 6/26/13

2.A.28

© 2013 Common Core, Inc. All rights reserved. **commoncore.org**

# A

# Correct _____

Fill-in the missing number.

| | | | | | | |
|---|---|---|---|---|---|---|
| 1 | 0 + | = 10 | 23 | 13 + | = | 20 |
| 2 | 9 + | = 10 | 24 | 23 + | = | 30 |
| 3 | 8 + | = 10 | 25 | 27 + | = | 30 |
| 4 | 7 + | = 10 | 26 | 5 + | = | 10 |
| 5 | 6 + | = 10 | 27 | 25 + | = | 30 |
| 6 | 5 + | = 10 | 28 | 2 + | = | 10 |
| 7 | 1 + | = 10 | 29 | 22 + | = | 30 |
| 8 | 2 + | = 10 | 30 | 32 + | = | 30 |
| 9 | 3 + | = 10 | 31 | 1 + | = | 10 |
| 10 | 4 + | = 10 | 32 | 11 + | = | 20 |
| 11 | 10 + | = 10 | 33 | 21 + | = | 30 |
| 12 | 9 + | = 10 | 34 | 31 + | = | 40 |
| 13 | 19 + | = 20 | 35 | 38 + | = | 40 |
| 14 | 5 + | = 10 | 36 | 36 + | = | 40 |
| 15 | 15 + | = 20 | 37 | 39 + | = | 40 |
| 16 | 8 + | = 10 | 38 | 35 + | = | 40 |
| 17 | 18 + | = 20 | 39 | + 6 | = | 30 |
| 18 | 6 + | = 10 | 40 | + 8 | = | 20 |
| 19 | 16 + | = 20 | 41 | + 7 | = | 40 |
| 20 | 7 + | = 10 | 42 | + 6 | = | 20 |
| 21 | 17 + | = 20 | 43 | + 4 | = | 30 |
| 22 | 3 + | = 10 | 44 | + 8 | = | 40 |

© Bill Davidson

**COMMON CORE** | Lesson 3: | Apply concepts to create unit rulers, measure lengths using unit rulers. | 2.A.29
| | Date: | 6/26/13 |

**B**

Improvement _____          # Correct _____

Fill-in the missing number.

| | | | | | | | |
|---|---|---|---|---|---|---|---|
| 1 | 10 + | = 10 | | 23 | 14 + | = | 20 |
| 2 | 9 + | = 10 | | 24 | 24 + | = | 30 |
| 3 | 8 + | = 10 | | 25 | 26 + | = | 30 |
| 4 | 7 + | = 10 | | 26 | 9 + | = | 10 |
| 5 | 6 + | = 10 | | 27 | 29 + | = | 30 |
| 6 | 5 + | = 10 | | 28 | 3 + | = | 10 |
| 7 | 1 + | = 10 | | 29 | 23 + | = | 30 |
| 8 | 2 + | = 10 | | 30 | 33 + | = | 30 |
| 9 | 3 + | = 10 | | 31 | 2 + | = | 10 |
| 10 | 4 + | = 10 | | 32 | 12 + | = | 20 |
| 11 | 0 + | = 10 | | 33 | 22 + | = | 30 |
| 12 | 5 + | = 10 | | 34 | 32 + | = | 40 |
| 13 | 15 + | = 20 | | 35 | 37 + | = | 40 |
| 14 | 9 + | = 10 | | 36 | 34 + | = | 40 |
| 15 | 19 + | = 20 | | 37 | 35 + | = | 40 |
| 16 | 8 + | = 10 | | 38 | 39 + | = | 40 |
| 17 | 18 + | = 20 | | 39 | + 4 | = | 30 |
| 18 | 7 + | = 10 | | 40 | + 9 | = | 20 |
| 19 | 17 + | = 20 | | 41 | + 4 | = | 40 |
| 20 | 6 + | = 10 | | 42 | + 7 | = | 20 |
| 21 | 16 + | = 20 | | 43 | + 3 | = | 30 |
| 22 | 4 + | = 10 | | 44 | + 9 | = | 40 |

© Bill Davidson

Lesson 3:  Apply concepts to create unit rulers, measure lengths using unit rulers.

Date:  6/26/13

2.A.30

Name _____    Date _____

Use your centimeter ruler to measure the length of the objects below.

1.  The picture of the animal track is about _____ cm long.

2.  The picture of the turtle is about _____ cm long.

3.  The picture of the sandwich is about _____ cm long.

4. Measure and label the length of each side of the triangle using your ruler.

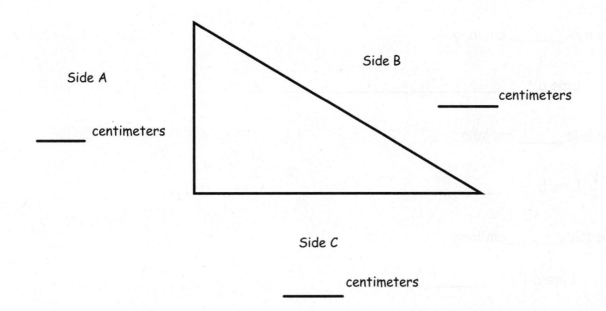

Side A

_____ centimeters

Side B

_____ centimeters

Side C

_____ centimeters

a. Which side is the shortest?   Side A          Side B          Side C

b. What is the length of Sides A and B together? _____ centimeters.

c. How much shorter is Side C than Side B? _____ centimeters.

Name _____    Date _____

1.  Use your centimeter ruler.  What is the length in centimeters of each line?

    a.  Line a is _____cm long.

        Line a        _____

    b.  Line b is _____cm long.

        Line b        _____

    c.  Line c is _____cm long.

        Line c        _____

2.  Find the length across the center of the circle.

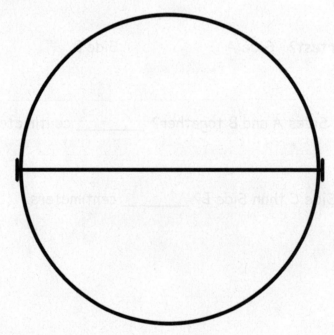

    The length across the circle is _____ cm.

Name _____     Date _____

Measure the lengths of the objects with the centimeter ruler you made in class.

1.  The picture of the fish is _____ cm long.

2.  The picture of the fish tank is _____ cm long.

3.  The picture of the fish tank is _____cm longer than the picture of the fish.

---

**COMMON CORE**™    **Lesson 3:**    Apply concepts to create unit rulers, measure lengths using unit
                    rulers.
            **Date:**        6/26/13

2.A.34

4.  Measure the lengths of sides A, B, and C.  Write their length on the line.

Side A

_____ cm

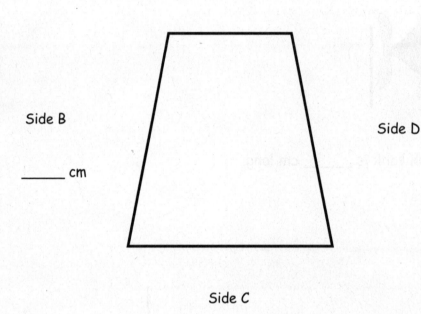

Side B

_____ cm

Side D

Side C

_____ cm

a.  Which side is the longest?        Side A        Side B        Side C

b.  How much longer is Side B than Side A? _____ cm longer.

c.  How much shorter is Side A than Side C? _____ cm shorter.

d.  Sides B and D are the same length.  What is the length of Sides B and D together?

    _____ cm.

e.  What is the total length of all four sides of this figure? _____ cm.

**COMMON CORE**™

Lesson 3:   Apply concepts to create unit rulers, measure lengths using unit
            rulers.
Date:       6/26/13

2.A.35

## Topic B

# Measure and Estimate Length Using Different Measurement Tools

## 2.MD.1, 2.MD.3

| Focus Standard: | 2.MD.1 | Measure the length of an object by selecting and using appropriate tools such as rulers, yardsticks, meter sticks, and measuring tapes. |
| --- | --- | --- |
| | 2.MD.3 | Estimate lengths using units of inches, feet, centimeters, and meters. |
| Instructional Days: | 2 | |
| Coherence  -Links from: | G1–M3 | Ordering and Comparing Length Measurement as Numbers |
| -Links to: | G2–M7 | Problem Solving with Length, Money, and Data |
| | G3–M2 | Place Value and Problem Solving with Units of Measure |

In Topic B, Lesson 4, students begin using centimeter rulers, meter sticks, and meter tapes to measure various objects.  Through the practice of measuring various items and learning mental benchmarks for measurement, students organically develop estimation skills in Lesson 5.  They also develop their skills for selecting an appropriate measuring tool by referencing prior knowledge of objects they have already measured, as well as by using mental benchmarks.

| A Teaching Sequence Towards Mastery of Measuring and Estimating Length Using Different Measurement Tools |
| --- |
| **Objective 1:** Measure various objects using centimeter rulers and meter sticks.<br>(Lesson 4) |
| **Objective 2:** Develop estimation strategies by applying prior knowledge of length and using mental benchmarks.<br>(Lesson 5) |

# Lesson 4

Objective:  Measure various objects using centimeter rulers and meter sticks.

## Suggested Lesson Structure

- ■ Fluency Practice          (13 minutes)
- ■ Application Problems       (7 minutes)
- ■ Concept Development        (30 minutes)
- ■ Student Debrief            (10 minutes)

    **Total Time**              **(60 minutes)**

## Fluency Practice  (13 minutes)

- ▪ Related Facts on a Ruler  **2.OA.2**        (4 minutes)
- ▪ Related Facts  **2.OA.2**                (9 minutes)

Note:  This fluency utilizes the ruler made in Lesson 3 to fluently review related facts.

## Related Facts on a Ruler  (4 minutes)

T:  Put your finger on 3 on the ruler you made yesterday.  Raise your hand when you know 8 more than 3.  Ready?

S:  11.

T:  Give a number sentence starting with 3 that shows 8 more.

S:  3 + 8 = 11.

T:  Give a number sentence to show 3 more than 8.

S:  8 + 3 = 11.

T:  Put your finger on 11.  Raise your hand when you know 3 less than 11.

S:  8.

T:  Number sentence?

S:  11 – 3 = 8.

T:  Give a number sentence to show 8 less than 11.

S:  11 – 8 = 3.

Continue with possible sequence:  9, 2, 11; 4, 9, 13; 8, 5, 13; 7, 5, 12; 9, 6, 15.

**NOTES ON
MULTIPLE MEANS OF
ACTION AND EXPRESSION:**

Provide support:

- ▪ Sprints are only 1 minute, but for students who don't excel under pressure, you may give them the chance to practice the sprint at home the night before it is administered.

- ▪ Guide personal goal-setting within a time frame (e.g., finish more problems correctly on the second sprint).  Have students ask, "How did I improve?"

- ▪ Allow the class to finish Sprint A after the minute has ended to help prepare for Sprint B.

Lesson 4:      Measure various objects using centimeter rulers and meter sticks.
Date:          6/26/13

2.B.2

## Sprint: Related Facts (9 minutes)

Materials: (S) Related Facts Sprint

## Application Problem (7 minutes)

Cameron wants to draw a canoe that is 16 centimeters long. He has 16 centimeter cubes, a centimeter ruler, and 16 paperclips of various sizes in his desk. Which measurement tool would you recommend for Cameron? Why? Write a sentence to explain your thinking.

*I would tell Cameron to use a cm. ruler because it's the easiest and quickest to use. Plus you can't use things that are different sizes.*

What if Cameron was asked to paint a much larger, life-size canoe as scenery for the school play? Is there any other way he could measure it? (Students share responses orally.)

Note: Today's problem asks students to synthesize their understanding of choosing an appropriate measurement tool, one that is accurate and efficient. Since students are being asked to write, assign them partners such that each partnership has a strong writer who is comfortable with language and vocabulary. Students then share their responses in small groups. Highlight one or two exemplary responses after small group sharing. The second portion of the problem sets the stage for the introduction of meter sticks and meter tape as another measurement tool

## Concept Development (30 minutes)

Materials: (S) Centimeter rulers made in Lesson 3, meter sticks, meter tape, one text book per student

T: Let's redecorate the room. I want to measure the carpet to see how long our new one should be.

T: Can someone bring his ruler up from yesterday to measure the carpet?

S: (Measures the carpet with centimeter ruler.)

T: That took a very long time! Maybe we should have used this! (Hold up the meter stick.)

T: Look at these tools I have! (Lay a meter stick and meter tape on the ground.) Can I have two volunteers lay some rulers down on top of the **meter stick** and the meter tape to measure their length in centimeters?

**MP.5**

T: How many centimeters are in one **meter**?

S: It is 100 cm. → It's just a little longer than 3 centimeter rulers.

T: This is another unit of measure called a meter. When we are measuring things that are more than 100 cm we can measure in meters.

T: We use a meter stick exactly the same way we use a ruler.

NOTES ON
MULTIPLE MEANS
OF ENGAGEMENT:

Assign students a *measurement discovery buddy* to clarify directions and/or processes. Buddies compare answers to check their work.

| Lesson 4: | Measure various objects using centimeter rulers and meter sticks. |
| Date: | 6/26/13 |

2.B.3

T:    (Call on a volunteer to measure the rug with a meter stick.)

T:    I notice that the rug is 4 meters and some more. When a measurement does not reach an exact measurement we have to round up or down to whichever number is closer.

T:    Since the rug is just a little more than 4 meters we can say it is *about* 4 meters long.

T:    We use the meter tape in exactly the same way. When would the meter tape be an appropriate measuring tool?

S:    When I am measuring my head. → When I am measuring something round. → When I am measuring something that is not straight.

**MP.5**

T:    I want to build a bookshelf for our science books. Let's use the centimeter rulers we made yesterday to measure the length of our books to see how high the shelf should be. Turn to your neighbor and estimate the length of your science book. (Students estimate.)

T:    Measure your science book from top to bottom. How high should my shelf be?

S:    (Share answers.)

T:    Now we need to see how long the shelf should be to hold all the books. (Call students up table by table to stack their books in one pile.)

T:    Which is the best tool to measure our stack of books?

S:    The meter stick or the meter tape!

T:    (Call on a student volunteer to measure the stack of books.)

T:    The bookshelf will need to be 20 cm high and 92 cm long. Work with your partner and use your measurement tools to measure spaces around the room. Where will the bookshelf fit?

S:    (Work in pairs to find a place for the bookshelf.)

T:    (Call students back together and share places the bookshelf could go.)

T:    Now you will have some time to continue planning for our redecoration. Measure objects around the room using an appropriate measuring tool. Record your measurements as you go. (Present Problem Set.)

## Problem Set (10 minutes)

Students should do their personal best to complete the Problem Set within the allotted 10 minutes. For some classes, it may be appropriate to modify the assignment by specifying which problems they work on first. Some problems do not specify a method for solving. Students solve these problems using the RDW approach used for Application Problems.

Name Zach        Date April 2, 2013

1. Measure 5 things in the classroom with a centimeter ruler. List the five things and their length in centimeters.

| Object Name | Length in centimeters |
|---|---|
| a. Book | 27 cm |
| b. post it | 8 cm |
| c. crayon | 9 cm |
| d. eraser | 5 cm |
| e. pencil sharpener | 3 cm |

2. Measure 4 things in the classroom with a meter stick or meter tape. List the four things and their length in meters.

| Object Name | Length in meters |
|---|---|
| a. door width | 1 m |
| b. rug | 2 m |
| c. teachers desk | 1 m |
| d. Bookcase | 2 m |

Lesson 4:    Measure various objects using centimeter rulers and meter sticks.
Date:       6/26/13

2.B.4

## Student Debrief  (10 minutes)

**Lesson Objective**:  Measure various objects using centimeter rulers and meter sticks.

The Student Debrief is intended to invite reflection and active processing of the total lesson experience.

Invite students to review their solutions for the Problem Set.  They should check work by comparing answers with a partner before going over answers as a class.  Look for misconceptions or misunderstandings that can be addressed in the Debrief.  Guide students in a conversation to debrief the Problem Set and process the lesson.  You may choose to use any combination of the questions below to lead the discussion.

Share with your partner:  Which things did you measure in centimeters?  Why?  Which things did you measure in meters?  Why?

- Did you or your partner disagree on any of the measurement tools you selected?  Defend your choice.

- How do the size and shape of what we measure tell us which tool is most appropriate?

- What new (or significant) math vocabulary have we learned?  (Chart student responses.  Prompt students to list vocabulary from the lesson such as measure, measurement, length, height, length unit, measuring tool, meter tape, **meter, meter stick,** etc.)

## Exit Ticket (3 minutes)

After the Student Debrief, instruct students to complete the Exit Ticket.  A review of their work will help you assess the students' understanding of the concepts that were presented in the lesson today and plan more effectively for future lessons.  You may read the questions aloud to the students.

**A**

# Correct _____

Add or subtract.

| | | | | | | |
|---|---|---|---|---|---|---|
| 1 | 8 + 3 = | | 23 | 15 - 6 = | |
| 2 | 3 + 8 = | | 24 | 15 - 9 = | |
| 3 | 11 - 3 = | | 25 | 8 + 7 = | |
| 4 | 11 - 8 = | | 26 | 7 + 8 = | |
| 5 | 7 + 4 = | | 27 | 15 - 7 = | |
| 6 | 4 + 7 = | | 28 | 15 - 8 = | |
| 7 | 11 - 4 = | | 29 | 9 + 4 = | |
| 8 | 11 - 7 = | | 30 | 4 + 9 = | |
| 9 | 9 + 3 = | | 31 | 13 - 4 = | |
| 10 | 3 + 9 = | | 32 | 13 - 9 = | |
| 11 | 12 - 3 = | | 33 | 8 + 6 = | |
| 12 | 12 - 9 = | | 34 | 6 + 8 = | |
| 13 | 8 + 5 = | | 35 | 14 - 6 = | |
| 14 | 5 + 8 = | | 36 | 14 - 8 = | |
| 15 | 13 - 5 = | | 37 | 7 + 6 = | |
| 16 | 13 - 8 = | | 38 | 6 + 7 = | |
| 17 | 7 + 5 = | | 39 | 13 - 6 = | |
| 18 | 5 + 7 = | | 40 | 13 - 7 = | |
| 19 | 12 - 5 = | | 41 | 9 + 7 = | |
| 20 | 12 - 7 = | | 42 | 7 + 9 = | |
| 21 | 9 + 6 = | | 43 | 16 - 7 = | |
| 22 | 6 + 9 = | | 44 | 16 - 9 = | |

© Bill Davidson

**COMMON CORE™**

Lesson 4: Measure various objects using centimeter rulers and meter sticks.
Date: 6/26/13

2.B.6

**B**

Add or subtract.

Improvement _____    # Correct _____

| | | | | | |
|---|---|---|---|---|---|
| 1 | 9 + 2 = | | 23 | 15 - 7 = | |
| 2 | 2 + 9 = | | 24 | 15 - 8 = | |
| 3 | 11 - 2 = | | 25 | 9 + 6 = | |
| 4 | 11 - 9 = | | 26 | 6 + 9 = | |
| 5 | 6 + 5 = | | 27 | 15 - 6 = | |
| 6 | 5 + 6 = | | 28 | 15 - 9 = | |
| 7 | 11 - 5 = | | 29 | 7 + 5 = | |
| 8 | 11 - 6 = | | 30 | 5 + 7 = | |
| 9 | 8 + 4 = | | 31 | 12 - 5 = | |
| 10 | 4 + 8 = | | 32 | 12 - 7 = | |
| 11 | 12 - 4 = | | 33 | 9 + 5 = | |
| 12 | 12 - 8 = | | 34 | 5 + 9 = | |
| 13 | 7 + 6 = | | 35 | 14 - 5 = | |
| 14 | 6 + 7 = | | 36 | 14 - 9 = | |
| 15 | 13 - 6 = | | 37 | 8 + 6 = | |
| 16 | 13 - 7 = | | 38 | 6 + 8 = | |
| 17 | 9 + 3 = | | 39 | 14 - 6 = | |
| 18 | 3 + 9 = | | 40 | 14 - 8 = | |
| 19 | 12 - 3 = | | 41 | 9 + 8 = | |
| 20 | 12 - 9 = | | 42 | 8 + 9 = | |
| 21 | 8 + 7 = | | 43 | 17 - 8 = | |
| 22 | 7 + 8 = | | 44 | 17 - 9 = | |

© Bill Davidson

Date:   6/26/13

Name _____  Date _____

1. Measure 5 things in the classroom with a centimeter ruler. List the five things and their length in centimeters.

| Object Name | Length in centimeters |
|---|---|
| a. | |
| b. | |
| c. | |
| d. | |
| e. | |

2. Measure 4 things in the classroom with a meter stick or meter tape. List the four things and their length in meters.

| Object Name | Length in meters |
|---|---|
| a. | |
| b. | |
| c. | |
| d. | |

COMMON CORE™

Lesson 4:    Measure various objects using centimeter rulers and meter sticks.
Date:        6/26/13

2.B.8

3. List 5 things in your house that you would measure with a meter stick or meter tape.

   1. _____

   2. _____

   3. _____

   4. _____

   5. _____

Why would you want to measure those five items with a meter stick or meter tape instead of a centimeter ruler?

_____

_____

4. The distance from the cafeteria to the gym is 14 meters. The distance from the cafeteria to the playground is double the distance. How many times would you need to use a meter stick to measure the distance from the cafeteria to the playground?

Name _____     Date _____

1. Circle centimeter or meter to show which measurement you would use to measure the length of each object.

   Length of a train            cm    or    m

   Length of an envelope       cm    or    m

   Length of a house          cm    or    m

2. Would it take more meters or more centimeters to measure the length of playground? Explain your answer.

   _____

   _____

   _____

Name _____     Date _____

1. Circle cm (centimeter) or m (meter) to show which measurement you would use to measure the length of each object.

    a.  Length of a marker              cm or m
    b.  Length of a school bus          cm or m
    c.  Length of a laptop computer     cm or m
    d.  Length of a highlighter marker  cm or m
    e.  Length of a football field      cm or m
    f.  Length of a parking lot         cm or m
    g.  Length of a cell phone          cm or m
    h.  Length of a lamp                cm or m
    i.   Length of a supermarket        cm or m
    j.  Length of a playground          cm or m


2. Fill in the blanks with **cm** or **m**.

    a.  The length of a swimming pool is 25 _____.

    b.  The height of a house is 8 _____.

    c.  Karen is 6 _____ shorter than her sister.

    d.  Eric ran 65 _____ down the street.

    e.  The length of a pencil box is 3 _____ longer than a pencil.

**COMMON CORE**   Lesson 4:   Measure various objects using centimeter rulers and meter sticks.
                  Date:       6/26/13

2.B.11

3. Use a centimeter ruler to find the length (from one hash mark to the next) of each object.

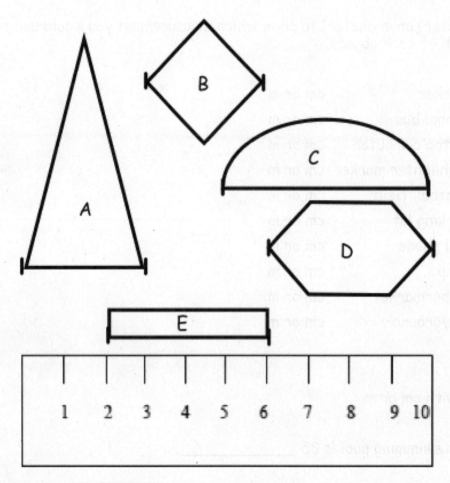

a. Triangle A is _____ cm long.          Square B is _____ cm long.

   Semi-circle C is _____ cm long.        Hexagon D is _____ cm long.

   Rectangle E is _____ cm long.

b. Explain how the strategy to find the length of each shape above is different than how you would find the length if you used a centimeter cube.

_____

_____

# Lesson 5

Objective:  Develop estimation strategies by applying prior knowledge of length and using mental benchmarks.

## Suggested Lesson Structure

■ Fluency Practice          (8 minutes)
■ Application Problems       (7 minutes)
■ Concept Development        (35 minutes)
■ Student Debrief           (10 minutes)
   **Total Time**          **(60 minutes)**

## Fluency Practice  (8 minutes)

- Break Apart by Tens and Ones  **2.NBT.1**          (4 minutes)
- Take Out a Part  **2.OA.2**          (4 minutes)

Note:  This fluency reviews place value understanding from Module 1 and helps develop skills needed for module 3.

### Break Apart by Tens and Ones  (4 minutes)

Materials:  (S) Personal white boards

   T:   If I say 64, you write 6 tens 4 ones.
   T:   If I say 7 tens 2 ones, you write 72.
   T:   Turn your board over when you've written your answer.  When I say, "Show me," hold it up.
   T:   5 tens 2 ones.  (Pause.)  Show me.
   S:   (Hold up boards showing 52.)
   T:   84.  (Pause.)  Show me.
   S:   (Show 8 tens 4 ones.)

Continue with possible sequence:  7 tens 3 ones, 79, 8 tens 9 ones, 9 tens 9 ones, 10 tens 2 ones, 10 tens 4 ones, 104, 10 tens 8 ones, 11 tens, 11 tens 5 ones.

   T:   Partner B, quiz Partner A for 1 minute.

Lesson 5:          Develop estimation strategies by applying prior knowledge
                   of length and using mental benchmarks.
Date:              6/26/13

2.B.13

## Take Out a Part  (4 minutes)

T:   Let's take out 2 tens from each number.

T:   I say 5 tens.  You say, 2 tens + 3 tens = 5 tens.

T:   5 tens.  Get ready.  (Signal.)

S:   2 tens + 3 tens = 5 tens.

T:   7 tens.  Get ready.  (Signal.)

S:   2 tens + 5 tens = 7 tens.

T:   Let's take out 20 from each number.

T:   I say 50.  You say, 20 + 30 = 50.

T:   50.  Get ready.  (Signal.)

S:   20 + 30 = 50.

T:   70.  Get ready.  (Signal.)

S:   20 + 50 = 70.

Continue with possible sequence:  83, 52, 97, 100, 105, 110, and 120.

T:   Now let's take out 40.  If I say 60, you say 40 + 20 = 60.

T:   50.  Wait for the signal (pause and signal).

S:   40 + 10 = 50.

Continue with possible sequence:  70, 75, 81, 87, etc.

## Application Problem  (7 minutes)

Jenna and Bobby are building a rope ladder for their treehouse.  They would like the ladder to be about the length of a sports car.  They want to use rope for the sides of the ladder and wooden rungs for the steps.  Which measurement tools would you suggest that Jenna and Bobby use to measure the length of the rope and the length of the rungs for their ladder?  Draw a picture and use words to explain your thinking.

*ladder*

*I would suggest a centimeter ruler for the rungs and a meter stick for the rope.*

Note: Today's problem asks students to choose the appropriate measurement tool by applying prior knowledge of length and making comparisons.  Students work independently using personal boards and then compare their responses with a partner.  The teacher listens in on conversations and invites a few students to share their responses with the whole class.  The teacher may wish to return to this problem during the debrief segment to estimate the amount of rope needed to build the ladder.

Lesson 5:  Develop estimation strategies by applying prior knowledge of length and using mental benchmarks.

Date:  6/26/13

**2.B.14**

# Concept Development (35 minutes)

Materials:  (T) Meter stick displayed horizontally for student reference  (S) 1 unsharpened brand new pencil
and 1 centimeter cube per student, student-created ruler from Lesson 3, meter tape one per
student

**MP.2**

T:  Put your pinky on your centimeter cube.  Would you
say it's about the same length as the centimeter cube?

S:  Yes.

T:  How could you use your pinky to estimate length?

S:  I can tell how many times my pinky would fit into the
space.  → I can put my pinky down as many times as I
can and then count.

T:  Let's try that.  Use your pinky to estimate, about how
long do you think the eraser is?  Turn to your neighbor
and share your estimate.

S:  About 6 centimeters.

T:  Let's measure to see if your estimates are correct.

S:  (Use student-created rulers to check estimates.)

T:  The distance from the floor to the doorknob is about
one meter (verify by modeling).  How does this help
you estimate the length of your desk?

S:  My desk is about half the length from the floor to the
doorknob.  So it's about 50 centimeters long.  → My
desk is twice the length from the floor to the doorknob
so I think it's about 2 meters long.

T:  Let's measure to see which estimate is closer to the
real measurement.

S:  (Use meter tapes to measure their desks.)

T:  Measure your pencil.  How long is it?

S:  About 20 centimeters.

T:  Can that help you estimate the length of your math
book?  Estimate the length of your math book and then
measure it with your centimeter ruler to see how close
you got.

S:  My math book is longer than the pencil, but not by
much.  → They are almost the same.  → I think it's
about 23 centimeters.  → I think it's 30 centimeters.

T:  Picture the meter stick in your mind.  Estimate how
many meters long the whiteboard is.

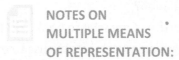

**NOTES ON
MULTIPLE MEANS
OF REPRESENTATION:**

During this lesson students will be
learning multiple benchmark
measurements.  To help all students
remember the benchmarks the
teacher may use these techniques:

- Partner language with visuals by
  posting pictures of the
  benchmarks.

- Instruct students to create a
  reference chart to keep track of
  the benchmarks as they learn
  them.  They can refer to this chart
  later as well.

**NOTES ON
MULTIPLE MEANS
OF ENGAGEMENT:**

Use a chant to help students
understand the conversion from
meters to centimeters. The teacher
adds gestures to accompany the
chant.

- T: When I say meter, you say 100
  centimeters. (Open arms wide,
  about the length of a meter.)

- T: Meter! (Open arms wide.)

- S: 100 centimeters ! (Open arms
  wide.)

This conversion is meant to support
students' estimations of the length
of their desks.

Lesson 5:    Develop estimation strategies by applying prior knowledge
of length and using mental benchmarks.
Date:    6/26/13

2.B.15

S: It looks like the board is a few meters long. → I can fit more than one meter stick along the length of the whiteboard. → I would say it is 2 meters long. → To me it's longer than 2 meters but shorter than 3 meters.

T: Let's check our estimates. (Call on a volunteer to measure the whiteboard for the class.)

T: Now look at this three-ring binder. What known measurement can we use to estimate the length?

S: It looks about the same as my ruler, so 30 centimeters.

**MP.2**

T: So let's check and see if it is 30 centimeters. (Student volunteer measures the three-ring binder.)

T: It is. Now that we know this is 30 centimeters what other lengths can we estimate with this information?

S: The length of my science book. → The length of the paper that goes inside the binder.

T: All these measurements we use to estimate length are called mental **benchmarks**. The pencil is 20 centimeters. Your pinky is 1 centimeter. The three-ring binder is 30 centimeters. And the length from the doorknob to the floor is 1 meter. You can use these benchmarks at any time by picturing them in your head to estimate the length of an object. Now use your mental benchmarks to estimate length on your worksheet. Check your estimates by measuring.

## Problem Set (10 minutes)

Students should do their personal best to complete the Problem Set within the allotted 10 minutes. For some classes, it may be appropriate to modify the assignment by specifying which problems they work on first. Some problems do not specify a method for solving. Students solve these problems using the RDW approach used for Application Problems.

## Student Debrief (10 minutes)

**Lesson Objective:** Develop estimation strategies by applying prior knowledge of length and using mental benchmarks.

The Student Debrief is intended to invite reflection and active processing of the total lesson experience.

Invite students to review their solutions for the Problem Set. They should check work by comparing answers with a partner before going over answers as a class. Look for misconceptions or misunderstandings that can be addressed in the Debrief. Guide students in a conversation to debrief the Problem Set and process the lesson.

You may choose to use any combination of the questions below to lead the discussion.

- Turn to your partner and compare your answers to Problems 1–5 in your Problem Set. Why is it possible to have different estimates? How can we check to see if our estimates are accurate?

Lesson 5: | Develop estimation strategies by applying prior knowledge
Date: | of length and using mental benchmarks.
6/26/13

2.B.16

- How many mental **benchmarks** can you name? (Draw students' attention to Problem 6 in their Problem Set.   Chart student responses for future reference.)

- How do mental benchmarks help us?  When is a good time to use them?

- (Return to today's application problem.)  Look at Problem 6(c) on your worksheet.  We said that the length of a car is about 4 meters.  How can we use this information to estimate the amount of rope Jenna and Bobby will need to build their ladder? 1

## Exit Ticket (3 minutes)

After the Student Debrief, instruct students to complete the Exit Ticket.  A review of their work will help you assess the students' understanding of the concepts that were presented in the lesson today and plan more effectively for future lessons.  You may read the questions aloud to the students.

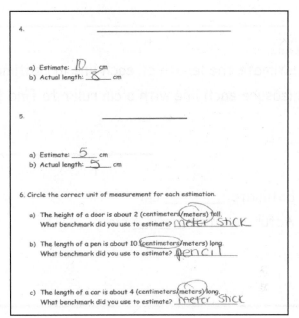

4. _____

a) Estimate: _10_ cm
b) Actual length: _8_ cm

5. _____

a) Estimate: _5_ cm
b) Actual length: _5_ cm

6. Circle the correct unit of measurement for each estimation.

a) The height of a door is about 2 (centimeters/meters) tall.
What benchmark did you use to estimate? meter stick

b) The length of a pen is about 10 (centimeters/meters) long.
What benchmark did you use to estimate? pencil

c) The length of a car is about 4 (centimeters/meters) long.
What benchmark did you use to estimate? meter stick

**NOTES ON MULTIPLE MEANS OF ACTION AND EXPRESSION:**

Provide sufficient wait time to allow students to process the connection between mental benchmarks and length of objects.

- Teacher points to or holds visuals while speaking.

Ask students to explain how and why they chose a specific mental benchmark when estimating length.

Lesson 5:     Develop estimation strategies by applying prior knowledge
Date:         of length and using mental benchmarks.
              6/26/13                                                          2.B.17

Name _____     Date _____

First estimate the length of each line in centimeters using mental benchmarks.
Then measure each line with a cm ruler to find the actual length.

1.     _____

    a. Estimate: _____ cm
    b. Actual length: _____ cm


2. _____

    a. Estimate: _____ cm
    b. Actual length: _____ cm


3.     _____

    a. Estimate: _____ cm
    b. Actual length: _____ cm


4.     _____

    a. Estimate: _____ cm
    b. Actual length: _____ cm

**Lesson 5:**    Develop estimation strategies by applying prior knowledge
              of length and using mental benchmarks.
**Date:**           6/26/13

2.B.18

5. _____

   a. Estimate: _____ cm
   b. Actual length: _____ cm

6. Circle the correct unit of measurement for each length estimation.

   a. The height of a door is about 2 (centimeters/meters) tall.
      What benchmark did you use to estimate? _____

   b. The length of a pen is about 10 (centimeters/meters) long.
      What benchmark did you use to estimate? _____

   c. The length of a car is about 4 (centimeters/meters) long.
      What benchmark did you use to estimate? _____

   d. The length of a bed is about 2 (centimeters/meters) long.
      What benchmark did you use to estimate? _____

   e. The length of a dinner plate is about 20 (centimeters/meters) long.
      What benchmark did you use to estimate? _____

7. Use an unsharpened pencil to estimate the length of 3 things in your desk.

   a. _____ is about _____ cm long.

   b. _____ is about _____ cm long.

   c. _____ is about _____ cm long.

Lesson 5:    Develop estimation strategies by applying prior knowledge
Date:        of length and using mental benchmarks.
             6/26/13

2.B.19

Name _____   Date _____

1. Circle the most reasonable estimate for each object.
   a. Length of a push pin              1 cm  or  1 m
   b. Length of classroom door          100 cm  or  2 m
   c. Length of a pair of students scissors   17 cm  or  42 cm

2. Estimate the length of your desk.  (Remember that your pinky is about 1 cm.)

   My desk is about _____ cm long.

3. How does knowing that an unsharpened pencil is about 20 cm long help you estimate
   the length of your arm from your elbow to your wrist?

   _____

   _____

COMMON
CORE™

Lesson 5:
Date:

Develop estimation strategies by applying prior knowledge
of length and using mental benchmarks.
6/26/13

2.B.20

Name _____    Date _____

1. Name 5 things in your home that you would measure in meters.
   Estimate their length.

   *Remember the length from a doorknob to the floor is about 1 meter.

| Item | Estimated Length |
|------|------------------|
| a. | |
| b. | |
| c. | |
| d. | |
| e. | |

2. Choose the best length estimate for each object.

a. Whiteboard          3 m        or      45 cm

b. Banana              12 cm      or      20 cm

c. DVD                 25 cm      or      17 cm

d. Pen                 18 cm      or      1 m

e. Swimming pool       50m        or      150 cm

Lesson 5:      Develop estimation strategies by applying prior knowledge
               of length and using mental benchmarks.
Date:          6/26/13

2.B.21

3. The width of your pinky finger is about 1 cm.
   Measure the length of the lines using your pinky finger. Write your estimation.


a. Line A _____

   Line A is about _____cm long.


b. Line B _____

   Line B is about _____cm long.


c. Line C _____

   Line C is about _____cm long.


d. Line D _____

   Line D is about _____cm long.


e. Line E _____

   Line E is about _____cm long.

Lesson 5:    Develop estimation strategies by applying prior knowledge
             of length and using mental benchmarks.
Date:        6/26/13

2.B.22

# Mathematics Curriculum

## Topic C

# Measure and Compare Lengths Using Different Length Units

## 2.MD.1, 2.MD.2, 2.MD.4

| | | |
|---|---|---|
| **Focus Standard:** | 2.MD.1 | Measure the length of an object by selecting and using appropriate tools such as rulers, yardsticks, meter sticks, and measuring tapes. |
| | 2.MD.2 | Measure the length of an object twice, using length units of different lengths for the two measurements; describe how the two measurements relate to the size of the unit chosen. |
| | 2.MD.4 | Measure to determine how much longer one object is than another, expressing the length difference in terms of a standard length unit. |
| **Instructional Days:** | 2 | |
| **Coherence   -Links from:** | GK–M3 | Comparison of Length, Weight, Capacity, and Numbers to 10 |
| | G1–M6 | Place Value, Comparison, Addition and Subtraction to 100 |
| **-Links to:** | G3–M2 | Place Value and Problem Solving with Units of Measure |
| | G3–M4 | Multiplication and Area |
| | G3–M7 | Geometry and Measurement Word Problems |

In Topic C, students use different length units to measure and compare lengths. In Lesson 6, they practice applying their knowledge of centimeters and meters to choose an appropriate measurement tool. They discover that there is a relationship between unit size and measurement when they measure one object twice using different length units. They learn that the larger the unit, the fewer number of units in a given measurement. In Lesson 7, students continue to measure and compare lengths using standard and non-standard length units. At this point students are prepared to explicitly compare different nonstandard length units and can make inferences about the relative size of objects.

**A Teaching Sequence Towards Mastery of Measuring and Comparing Lengths Using Different Length Units**

**Objective 1:** Measure and compare lengths using centimeters and meters.
(Lesson 6)

**Objective 2:** Measure and compare lengths using standard metric length units and nonstandard length units; relate measurement to unit size.
(Lesson 7)

# Lesson 6

Objective: Measure and compare lengths using centimeters and meters.

## Suggested Lesson Structure

■ Fluency Practice          (11 minutes)
■ Application Problems       (7 minutes)
■ Concept Development        (32 minutes)
■ Student Debrief           (10 minutes)

  **Total Time**            **(60 minutes)**

## Fluency Practice  (11 minutes)

- Happy Counting  **2.NBT.2**                 (2 minutes)
- Find the Longer Length  **2.NBT.4**         (9 minutes)

## Happy Counting  (2 minutes)

Note:  Students fluently count by tens crossing the hundred and relate it to metric units.

   T:   Let's do some Happy Counting in centimeters.  Watch me as I pinch the meter stick where the centimeters are while we count.  When I get to 100 centimeters (1 meter), I will call a volunteer to hold another the meter stick.

   T:   Let's count by tens, starting at 70 centimeters.  When we get to 100 centimeters, we say 1 meter, and then we will go back to counting by centimeters.  Ready?  (Pinch the meter stick to stop on a number, moving pinched fingers up and down to lead students in Happy Counting by tens on the meter stick.)

   S:   70 cm, 80 cm, 90 cm, 1 m, 110 cm, 120 cm (stop), 110 cm, 1 m, 90 cm, 80 cm (stop), 90 cm, 1 m, 110 cm, 120 cm (stop).

   T:   Now let's say it with meters and centimeters.  Let's start at 80 centimeters.  Ready?

   S:   80 cm, 90 cm, 1 m, 1 m 10 cm, 1 m 20 cm, 1 m 30 cm, 1 m 40 cm (top) 1 m 30 cm, 1 m 20 cm (stop) 1 m 30 cm, 1 m 40 cm, 1 m 50 cm, 1 m 60 cm, 1 m 70 cm, 1 m 80 cm, 1 m 90 cm, 2 m (stop).

## Sprint:  Find the Longer Length  (9 minutes)

Materials:  (S) Find the Longer Length Sprint

Note:  Students prepare for comparing lengths in the lesson by identifying the longer length in a sprint.

## Application Problems  (7 minutes)

Eve builds a block tower that reaches the height of her bedroom doorknob, which is one meter high.  Her little sister knocks some blocks down.  Eve measures her new tower, and it is 48 centimeters tall.  How does Eve's new tower compare to when it was first built?  Draw a picture on your personal board and use numbers or words to explain your thinking.

Note: Yesterday, students used mental benchmarks to estimate various lengths.  This problem connects the concept of mental benchmarks to the language of comparisons.  The question above is open-ended in nature; thus, student responses may vary from simple comparisons (e.g., it's smaller now.) to exact calculations, or even to the observation that it is now about half the size of the original tower.  This problem serves as a bridge to today's lesson, where students are asked to measure and compare various lengths to determine which is longer and which is shorter.

**NOTES ON MULTIPLE MEANS OF ACTION AND EXPRESSION:**

Couple comparative vocabulary with illustrative gestures and questions such as the following:

- Who is taller?  Shorter? (Students stand back to back.)
- How wide is this shoe?  How long?  Which shoe is longer? Which shoe is shorter?
- Point to visuals while speaking to highlight the vocabulary that corresponds with words.

## Concept Development  (32 minutes)

Materials:  (S) Centimeter rulers and meter strips, stapler, two sheets of loose leaf paper per pair of students

T:   I want to know:  How long is the paper?  (Students measure.)

T:   With your pencil, label this side (pointing) A.

S:   (Write an A along the length of the paper.)

T:   How wide is the paper?  (Students measure.)

T:   Label this side (pointing) B.

S:   (Students write a B along the width of the paper.)

T:   Which side is longer, side A or side B?

S:   Side A.

T:   How can I find out how much longer?  Figure out a way with your partner.

S:   Put two of them next to each other and see.  → You could measure.  → Measure and subtract.

T:   Go to your seat with your partner and find out:  How much longer is Side A than Side B?

Students go to their seats with two pieces of paper and solve the problem.  Allow 2–3 minutes for students to complete the task.  Observe student strategies to choose who will share.  Select 2–3 students who use different approaches to share with the class.

MP.2

T:   Who would like to share the strategy they used?

S:   I lined up the two papers and measured the piece that was sticking out.  → I measured both sides and counted on.

T:   What strategy could you use if you only had one piece of paper?

S:   Measure and add on!  → Measure and subtract!

T:   (Teacher models measuring the difference in length using both strategies.)

Repeat the process above using the **meter strips** to measure and compare the lengths of other objects around the room (e.g., desks and whiteboard, the width of the door and the height of the door, the length of a bookcase and the height of a bookcase, student desk and teacher desk).  Allow students to record their measurements and work on their personal boards or in their math journals. Then have students complete the Problem Set.

## Problem Set  (10 minutes)

Students should do their personal best to complete the Problem Set within the allotted 10 minutes.  For some classes, it may be appropriate to modify the assignment by specifying which problems they work on first.  Some problems do not specify a method for solving.  Students solve these problems using the RDW approach used for Application Problems.

## Student Debrief  (10 minutes)

**Lesson Objective**: Measure and compare lengths using centimeters and meters.

The Student Debrief is intended to invite reflection and active processing of the total lesson experience.

Invite students to review their solutions for the Problem Set.  They should check work by comparing answers with a partner before going over answers as a class. Look for misconceptions or misunderstandings that can be addressed in the Debrief.  Guide students in a conversation to debrief the Problem Set and process the lesson.

### NOTES ON MULTIPLE MEANS OF ENGAGEMENT:

The language of comparisons may be particularly challenging for ELLs. The teacher can scaffold understanding of Problem 5 in the Problem Set using these techniques:

- Break down the problem into small, workable chunks (e.g., "If Alice's ribbon is 1 meter long, how many centimeters long is her ribbon?").

- Reframe the comparing sentence (e.g., "How much *more* ribbon does Alice have than Carol?").

- Teach students to ask themselves questions:  "What type of problem is this?  What do I know? What is unknown?"

These scaffolds will support Problem 6 on the Problem Set.

You may choose to use any combination of the questions below to lead the discussion.

- For Problems 1–3, discuss with your partner how you determined the difference in length of the lines you measured. What is interesting about line F in Problem 3?

- How did finding the missing addend in Problem 4 help you to answer Problem 5?

- Explain to your partner how you solved Problem 6 or Problem 7. How did you show your thinking?

- When you were measuring the paper today, how did your strategy change the second time you solved the problem? Which strategy was more efficient and accurate?

- How would you convince me that there is a benefit to measuring with centimeters versus meters? How about a ruler versus a **meter strip**?

## Exit Ticket (3 minutes)

After the Student Debrief, instruct students to complete the Exit Ticket. A review of their work will help you assess the students' understanding of the concepts that were presented in the lesson today and plan more effectively for future lessons. You may read the questions aloud to the students.

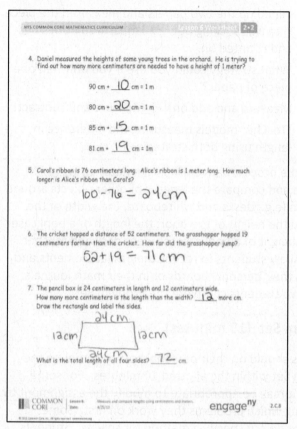

COMMON CORE | Lesson 6: | Measure and compare lengths using centimeters and meters.
Date: | 6/26/13

2.C.6

# A

# Correct _____

Circle the longer length.

| | | | | | | |
|---|---|---|---|---|---|---|
| 1 | 1 cm | 0 cm | | 23 | 110 cm | 101 cm |
| 2 | 11 cm | 10 cm | | 24 | 110 cm | 1 m |
| 3 | 11 cm | 12 cm | | 25 | 1 m | 111 cm |
| 4 | 22 cm | 12 cm | | 26 | 101 cm | 1 m |
| 5 | 29 cm | 30 cm | | 27 | 111 cm | 101 cm |
| 6 | 31 cm | 13 cm | | 28 | 112 cm | 102 cm |
| 7 | 43 cm | 33 cm | | 29 | 110 cm | 115 cm |
| 8 | 33 cm | 23 cm | | 30 | 115 cm | 105 cm |
| 9 | 35 cm | 53 cm | | 31 | 106 cm | 116 cm |
| 10 | 50 cm | 35 cm | | 32 | 108 cm | 98 cm |
| 11 | 55 cm | 45 cm | | 33 | 119 cm | 99 cm |
| 12 | 50 cm | 55 cm | | 34 | 131 cm | 133 cm |
| 13 | 65 cm | 56 cm | | 35 | 133 cm | 113 cm |
| 14 | 66 cm | 56 cm | | 36 | 142 cm | 124 cm |
| 15 | 66 cm | 86 cm | | 37 | 144 cm | 114 cm |
| 16 | 86 cm | 68 m | | 38 | 154 cm | 145 cm |
| 17 | 68 cm | 88 cm | | 39 | 155 cm | 152 cm |
| 18 | 89 cm | 98 cm | | 40 | 198 cm | 199 cm |
| 19 | 99 cm | 98 m | | 41 | 215 cm | 225 cm |
| 20 | 99 cm | 1 m | | 42 | 252 cm | 255 cm |
| 21 | 1 m | 101 cm | | 43 | 2 m | 295 cm |
| 22 | 1 m | 90 cm | | 44 | 3 m | 295 cm |

**Lesson 6:**
**Date:** 6/26/13

Measure and compare lengths using centimeters and meters.

2.C.7

**B**                          Improvement _____          # Correct _____

Circle the longer length.

| | | | | | |
|---|---|---|---|---|---|
| 1 | 0 cm | 1 cm | 23 | 111 cm | 101 cm |
| 2 | 10 cm | 12 cm | 24 | 101 cm | 110 cm |
| 3 | 12 cm | 11 cm | 25 | 1 m | 110 cm |
| 4 | 32 cm | 13 cm | 26 | 111 cm | 1 m |
| 5 | 39 cm | 40 cm | 27 | 113 cm | 117 cm |
| 6 | 41 cm | 14 cm | 28 | 112 cm | 111 cm |
| 7 | 44 cm | 40 cm | 29 | 115 cm | 105 cm |
| 8 | 44 cm | 54 cm | 30 | 106 cm | 116 cm |
| 9 | 55 cm | 65 cm | 31 | 107 cm | 117 cm |
| 10 | 60 cm | 59 cm | 32 | 118 cm | 108 cm |
| 11 | 65 cm | 45 cm | 33 | 119 cm | 120 cm |
| 12 | 70 cm | 65 cm | 34 | 132 cm | 123 cm |
| 13 | 75 cm | 57 cm | 35 | 133 cm | 132 cm |
| 14 | 77 cm | 76 cm | 36 | 143 cm | 134 cm |
| 15 | 87 cm | 78 cm | 37 | 144 cm | 114 cm |
| 16 | 79 cm | 97 m | 38 | 154 cm | 145 cm |
| 17 | 79 cm | 88 cm | 39 | 155 cm | 152 cm |
| 18 | 98 cm | 97 cm | 40 | 195 cm | 199 cm |
| 19 | 99 cm | 1 m | 41 | 225 cm | 152 cm |
| 20 | 99 cm | 100 cm | 42 | 252 cm | 255 cm |
| 21 | 101 cm | 100 cm | 43 | 2 m | 295 cm |
| 22 | 1 m | 101 cm | 44 | 3 m | 295 cm |

**COMMON CORE**      **Lesson 6:**     Measure and compare lengths using centimeters and meters.
                     **Date:**         6/26/13

2.C.8

Name _____    Date _____

Measure each set of lines in centimeters write the length on the line.  Complete the comparison sentence.

1.  Line A _____

Line B _____

Line A measured about _____ cm.        Line B measured about _____ cm.

Line A is about _____ cm longer than Line B.

2.  Line C            _____

Line D            _____

Line C measured about _____ cm.        Line D measured about _____ cm.

Line C is about _____ cm shorter than Line D.

3.  Line E _____

Line F                          _____

Line G            _____

Line E measured about _____ cm.    Line F measured about _____ cm.

Line G measured about _____ cm.    Lines E, F, and G are about_____ cm combined.

Line E is about _____ cm shorter than Line F.

Line E is about _____cm shorter than Line G.

Line G is about_____ cm longer than Line F.

Line F doubled is about _____cm longer than Line G.

4. Daniel measured the heights of some young trees in the orchard. He is trying to find out how many more centimeters are needed to have a height of 1 meter?

$$90 \text{ cm} + \underline{\hspace{1cm}} \text{ cm} = 1 \text{ m}$$

$$80 \text{ cm} + \underline{\hspace{1cm}} \text{ cm} = 1 \text{ m}$$

$$85 \text{ cm} + \underline{\hspace{1cm}} \text{ cm} = 1 \text{ m}$$

$$81 \text{ cm} + \underline{\hspace{1cm}} \text{ cm} = 1 \text{m}$$

5. Carol's ribbon is 76 centimeters long. Alice's ribbon is 1 meter long. How much longer is Alice's ribbon than Carol's?

6. The cricket hopped a distance of 52 centimeters. The grasshopper hopped 19 centimeters farther than the cricket. How far did the grasshopper jump?

COMMON CORE

Lesson 6:      Measure and compare lengths using centimeters and meters.
Date:          6/26/13

2.C.10

7.  The pencil box is 24 centimeters in length and 12 centimeters wide.  How many more centimeters is the length than the width? _____ more cm.

    Draw the rectangle and label the sides.

    What is the total length of all four sides? _____ cm.

Name _____  Date _____

1. Measure the length of each line and compare.

_____  Line M

_____  Line N

_____  Line O

Line M is about _____cm longer than Line O.

Line N is about _____cm shorter than Line M.

Line N doubled would be about _____cm (longer/shorter) than Line M.

Name _____    Date _____

Compare the lengths and complete each sentence.

1. _____ Line A

          _____ Line B

    Line A is about _____ cm longer than line B.

    Line A and B are about _____ cm combined.


2. _____ Line X

          _____ Line Y

                 _____ Line Z

    Line X measured about _____ cm.

    Line Y measured about _____ cm.

    Line Z measured about _____ cm.

    Lines X, Y, and Z are about_____ cm combined.

    Line Z is about _____ cm shorter than Line X.

    Line X is about _____cm shorter than Line Y.

    Line Y is about _____ cm longer than Line Z.

    Line X doubled is about _____cm longer than line Y.

3. Line J is 60 cm long.

   Line K is 85 cm long.

   Line L is 1 m long.

   Line J is _____ cm shorter than line K.

   Line L is _____ cm longer than line K.

   Line J doubled is _____ cm more than line L.

   Lines J, K, and L combined are _____ cm.

4. Katie measured the seat height of four different chairs in her house.

   Here are her results:
   Loveseat height: 51 cm                    Bar stool height: 97 cm
   Dining room chair height: 55 cm           Counter stool height: 65 cm

   a. How much shorter is the dining chair than the counter stool? _____ cm

   b. How much taller is the bar stool than the loveseat? _____ cm

   c. What is the difference between the height of tallest chair and the height of the shortest chair? _____ cm

   d. How much taller is a meter stick than the counter stool? _____ cm

   e. How much taller is a meter stick than the loveseat? _____ cm

**COMMON CORE**

Lesson 6:    Measure and compare lengths using centimeters and meters.
Date:        6/26/13

2.C.14

5. Max ran 15 meters this morning. This afternoon he ran 48 meters.
   a. How many more meters did he run in the afternoon?




   b. How many meters did Max run in all?




6. The length of the tabletop is 2 meters long. If the tablecloth on the table is 256 centimeters, how much longer is the tablecloth than the tabletop?

COMMON CORE

Lesson 6:     Measure and compare lengths using centimeters and meters.
Date:         6/26/13

2.C.15

# Lesson 7

Objective:  Measure and compare lengths using standard metric length units and non-standard lengths units; relate measurement to unit size.

## Suggested Lesson Structure

■ Fluency Practice          (11 minutes)
■ Application Problems       (6 minutes)
☐ Concept Development        (33 minutes)
■ Student Debrief           (10 minutes)
  **Total Time**            **(60 minutes)**

## Fluency Practice  (11 minutes)

- Which is Shorter?  **2.MD.4**          (2 minutes)
- Subtraction  **2.NBT.5**              (9 minutes)

### Which is Shorter?  (2 minutes)

Note:  Students prepare for comparing lengths by identifying the shorter length and providing the number sentence to find the difference.

  T:  I am going to say two lengths.  Tell me which length is shorter.  Ready?  6 centimeters and 10 centimeters.
  S:  6 centimeters.
  T:  Give the number sentence to find how much shorter.
  S:  10 cm – 6 cm = 4 cm.

Continue with the following possible sequence:  12 cm and 22 cm, 16 cm and 20 cm, 20 cm and 13 cm, 20 cm and 9 cm, 9 cm and 19 cm, 24 cm and 14 cm, 12 cm and 24 cm, 23 cm and 15 cm, 18 cm and 29 cm.

### Sprint:  Subtraction  (9 minutes)

Materials:  (S) Subtraction Sprint

Note:  Students practice their simple subtraction skills in preparation for the lesson content.

 Lesson 7:  Measure and compare lengths using standard metric length units and non-standard lengths units; relate measurement to unit size.
Date:  6/26/13

2.C.16

© 2013 Common Core, Inc. All rights reserved. commoncore.org

## Application Problem  (6 minutes)

Natalia, Chloe, and Lucas are making clay snakes.  Natalia's snake is 16 centimeters.  Chloe's snake is 5 centimeters shorter than Natalia's.  How long is Chloe's snake?  Draw a picture and use numbers to explain your thinking.

Lucas's snake is 3 centimeters longer than Chloe's snake.  Who has the longest snake:  Natalia, Lucas, or Chloe?  Add to your picture and use numbers to explain your thinking.

Note:  This two-step problem presents a challenge for students to extend their understanding of measuring and comparing.  Students are asked to connect addition and subtraction concepts to comparison language and to draw a conclusion.

## Concept Development  (33 minutes)

Materials:  (S) baggies with 1 straw, 1 new crayon, 1 pink eraser, 1 square post-it note, 30 paper clips (half of the baggies with small paper clips and half the baggies with large paper clips), 1 baggie per pair of students (only one size paper clip per table so students don't see that there are different sizes)

T:  Measure your straw with your paper clips.

S:  (Students measure.)

T:  How long is the straw?

S:  6 paper clips long. → About 4 and a half paper clips long.

T:  (Record measurements on the board.)

T:  Why do you think the measurements are different?  Turn and talk.

S:  Maybe they didn't start at the beginning of the straw. → They measured wrong.

T:  Take out your crayon and measure with your paper clips.  Share your measurement with your partner.

**NOTES ON MULTIPLE MEANS OF REPRESENTATION:**

Extend thinking by connecting to real world experiences.  Ask students, "What are some other items you might use to measure your straw?"  Students will identify objects that are easy to use as a measure:  erasers, fingers, crayons, etc. either by using mark and advance or by laying multiple copies.

Students continue to measure the other items in their baggies.  After each item discuss and record the unit measure (in paper clips) of each item.  Notice that measurements are different, but do not explain why.

**P.3**

T:  Let's switch baggies with our neighbors and measure again.

T:  (Tables now switch bags and measure all items in the baggie using the other size paper clip.  Teacher records measurements on the board.  Students discuss the difference between the measurements using the large paper clips and those using the small paper clips.)

T:  Do you know why your measurements were different?

S:  We had different sized paper clips!

T:  Why does the size of my paper clip matter?

**COMMON CORE**

Lesson 7:    Measure and compare lengths using standard metric length units and non-standard lengths units; relate measurement to unit size.

Date:    6/26/13

2.C.17

S: You can fit more small paper clips than big paper clips along the side of the item.

T: What does that tell you about measurement and unit size?

S: If it's a small unit size you get a bigger measurement number.

T: Let's measure again using small and big paper clips mixed together.

**MP.3**

S: (Students use varying amounts of small and big paper clips to measure their straws.)

T: What were your results? (Record results.)

T: Why are all these measurements different?

S: We all had different sizes. → Some people had lots of big paper clips.

T: So if I wanted to order a table and I told you I want it to be 80 paper clips long, what might happen?

S: They wouldn't know which one you want. → You could get a big table or a tiny table.

T: (Pass out different types of centimeter rulers, e.g. tape measures, wooden rulers, plastic rulers. Have students re-measure each object in their baggies. Record the measurements on the board in centimeters.)

T: What do you notice about the measurement of the object when you use a centimeter ruler?

S: The measurements for each object are the same even if the ruler looks different.

T: What is the same about all the rulers?

S: They are the same except one is wood and one is plastic. → The rulers all have centimeters. → The centimeters are all the same size.

T: Why is it more efficient to measure with a centimeter instead of paper clips?

S: Because everyone knows how big a centimeter is. → All centimeters are the same.

## Problem Set  (10 minutes)

Students should do their personal best to complete the Problem Set within the allotted 10 minutes. For some classes, it may be appropriate to modify the assignment by specifying which problems they work on first. Some problems do not specify a method for solving. Students solve these problems using the RDW approach used for Application Problems.

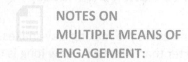

**NOTES ON MULTIPLE MEANS OF ENGAGEMENT:**

Inverse relationships require understanding, because they seem to challenge logic and reasoning.

Post sentence frames for ELLs to reference during the debrief: "The _____ the unit, the _____ number of units in a given measurement."

Invite students to brainstorm real-life examples of inverse relationships (e.g., The longer you sleep in the morning, the less time you have to get ready for school.).

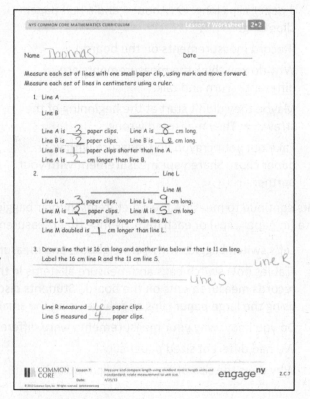

Lesson 7:    Measure and compare lengths using standard metric length units and non-standard lengths units; relate measurement to unit size.
Date:        6/26/13

2.C.18

© 2013 Common Core, Inc. All rights reserved. commoncore.org

## Student Debrief  (10 minutes)

**Lesson Objective**:  Measure and compare lengths using centimeters and meters; relate measurement to unit size.

The Student Debrief is intended to invite reflection and active processing of the total lesson experience.

Invite students to review their solutions for the Problem Set.  They should check work by comparing answers with a partner before going over answers as a class.  Look for misconceptions or misunderstandings that can be addressed in the Debrief.  Guide students in a conversation to debrief the Problem Set and process the lesson.  You may choose to use any combination of the questions below to lead the discussion.

Turn to your partner and compare your answers to Problems 1–4 on your worksheet.  Which math strategies did you use to determine which line was longer or shorter?

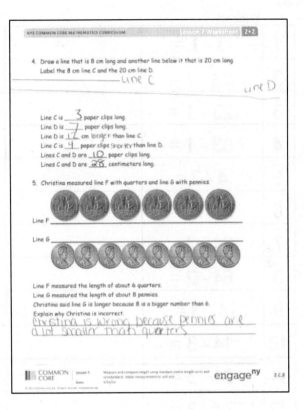

- Look at Problem 5 on your Problem Set.  Turn and talk to your partner about why Christina's answer is incorrect.

- Do you think that paperclips are a reliable measurement tool?  Is a ruler a better measurement tool? Why?

- What did you notice about the relationship between the unit of length (e.g., paper clips, centimeters) and the number of units needed to measure the lines?  Use comparative words (*bigger, smaller, greater, fewer*) in your response

- Let's think back to our application problem.  Would it have been possible to accurately compare the lengths of the clay snakes with a nonstandard length unit?  What challenges can you predict?

## Exit Ticket (3 minutes)

After the Student Debrief, instruct students to complete the Exit Ticket.  A review of their work will help you assess the students' understanding of the concepts that were presented in the lesson today and plan more effectively for future lessons.  You may read the questions aloud to the students.

## A

Subtract.

# Correct _____

| | | | | | |
|---|---|---|---|---|---|
| 1 | 3 - 1 = | | 23 | 8 - 7 = | |
| 2 | 13 - 1 = | | 24 | 18 - 7 = | |
| 3 | 23 - 1 = | | 25 | 58 - 7 = | |
| 4 | 53 - 1 = | | 26 | 62 - 2 = | |
| 5 | 4 - 2 = | | 27 | 9 - 8 = | |
| 6 | 14 - 2 = | | 28 | 19 - 8 = | |
| 7 | 24 - 2 = | | 29 | 29 - 8 = | |
| 8 | 64 - 2 = | | 30 | 69 - 8 = | |
| 9 | 4 - 3 = | | 31 | 7 - 3 = | |
| 10 | 14 - 3 = | | 32 | 17 - 3 = | |
| 11 | 24 - 3 = | | 33 | 77 - 3 = | |
| 12 | 74 - 3 = | | 34 | 59 - 9 = | |
| 13 | 6 - 4 = | | 35 | 9 - 7 = | |
| 14 | 16 - 4 = | | 36 | 19 - 7 = | |
| 15 | 26 - 4 = | | 37 | 89 - 7 = | |
| 16 | 96 - 4 = | | 38 | 99 - 5 = | |
| 17 | 7 - 5 = | | 39 | 78 - 6 = | |
| 18 | 17 - 5 = | | 40 | 58 - 5 = | |
| 19 | 27 - 5 = | | 41 | 39 - 7 = | |
| 20 | 47 - 5 = | | 42 | 28 - 6 = | |
| 21 | 43 - 3 = | | 43 | 49 - 4 = | |
| 22 | 87 - 7 = | | 44 | 67 - 4 = | |

© Bill Davidson

Lesson 7:  Measure and compare lengths using standard metric length units
and non-standard lengths units; relate measurement to unit size.
Date:  6/26/13

2.C.20

**B**

Subtract.

Improvement _____          # Correct _____

| | | | | | |
|---|---|---|---|---|---|
| 1 | 2 - 1 = | | 23 | 8 - 7 = | |
| 2 | 12 - 1 = | | 24 | 18 - 7 = | |
| 3 | 22 - 1 = | | 25 | 68 - 7 = | |
| 4 | 52 - 1 = | | 26 | 32 - 2 = | |
| 5 | 5 - 2 = | | 27 | 9 - 8 = | |
| 6 | 15 - 2 = | | 28 | 19 - 8 = | |
| 7 | 25 - 2 = | | 29 | 29 - 8 = | |
| 8 | 65 - 2 = | | 30 | 79 - 8 = | |
| 9 | 4 - 3 = | | 31 | 8 - 4 = | |
| 10 | 14 - 3 = | | 32 | 18 - 4 = | |
| 11 | 24 - 3 = | | 33 | 78 - 4 = | |
| 12 | 84 - 3 = | | 34 | 89 - 9 = | |
| 13 | 7 - 4 = | | 35 | 9 - 7 = | |
| 14 | 17 - 4 = | | 36 | 19 - 7 = | |
| 15 | 27 - 4 = | | 37 | 79 - 7 = | |
| 16 | 97 - 4 = | | 38 | 89 - 5 = | |
| 17 | 6 - 5 = | | 39 | 68 - 6 = | |
| 18 | 16 - 5 = | | 40 | 48 - 5 = | |
| 19 | 26 - 5 = | | 41 | 29 - 7 = | |
| 20 | 46 - 5 = | | 42 | 38 - 6 = | |
| 21 | 23 - 3 = | | 43 | 59 - 4 = | |
| 22 | 67 - 7 = | | 44 | 77 - 4 = | |

© Bill Davidson

**COMMON CORE™**

Lesson 7:   Measure and compare lengths using standard metric length units
and non-standard lengths units; relate measurement to unit size.

Date:       6/26/13

**2.C.21**

Name _____   Date _____

Measure each set of lines with one small paper clip, using mark and move forward.
Measure each set of lines in centimeters using a ruler.

1.  Line A _____

    Line B                     _____

    Line A is _____ paper clips.  Line A is _____ cm long.

    Line B is _____ paper clips.  Line B is _____ cm long.

    Line B is _____ paper clips shorter than Line A.

    Line A is _____ cm longer than Line B.

2.  _____ Line L

                     _____ Line M

    Line L is _____ paper clips.  Line L is _____ cm long.

    Line M is _____ paper clips. Line M is _____ cm long.

    Line L is _____ paper clips longer than Line M.

    Line M doubled is _____ cm longer than Line L.

3.  Draw a line that is 16 cm long and another line below it that is 11 cm long.
    Label the 16-cm line R and the 11-cm line S.


    Line R measured _____ paper clips.
    Line S measured _____ paper clips.

| | Lesson 7: | Measure and compare lengths using standard metric length units and non-standard lengths units; relate measurement to unit size. |
| --- | --- | --- |
| | Date: | 6/26/13 |

2.C.22

4. Draw a line that is 8 cm long and another line below it that is 20 cm long.

   Label the 8-cm line C and the 20-cm line D.



   Line C is _____ paper clips long.

   Line D is _____ paper clips long.

   Line D is _____ cm longer than Line C.

   Line C is _____ paper clips shorter than Line D.

   Lines C and D are _____ paper clips long.

   Lines C and D are _____ centimeters long.

5. Christina measured line F with quarters and line G with pennies.

   Line F _____

   Line G _____

   Line F measured the length of about 6 quarters.

   Line G measured the length of about 8 pennies.

   Christina said line G is longer because 8 is a bigger number than 6.

   Explain why Christina is incorrect.

   _____

   _____

**COMMON CORE™**     Lesson 7:     Measure and compare lengths using standard metric length units
                                    and non-standard lengths units; relate measurement to unit size.          **2.C.23**
                     Date:          6/26/13

Name _____ Date _____

Measure the lines with small paper clips and answer the questions below.

Line 1 _____

Line 2 _____

Line 3 _____

Line 1 is _____ paper clips.  Line 1 is _____ cm long.

Line 2 is _____ paper clips.  Line 2 is _____ cm long.

Line 3 is _____ paper clips.  Line 3 is _____ cm long.

Explain why each line had more centimeters than paper clips.

_____

_____

_____

**COMMON CORE**™

**Lesson 7:** Measure and compare lengths using standard metric length units and non-standard lengths units; relate measurement to unit size.
**Date:** 6/26/13

2.C.24

Name _____    Date _____

Use a centimeter ruler and paper clips to measure and compare lengths.

1.  _____ Line Z

    Line Z is _____ paper clips.  Line Z is _____ cm long.

    Line Z doubled would measure _____ paper clips or _____cm.

2.  _____ Line A

    _____ Line B

    Line A is _____ paper clips.  Line A is _____ cm long.

    Line B is _____ paper clips.  Line B is _____ cm long.

    Line A is _____ paper clips longer than Line B.

    Line B doubled is _____ cm longer than Line A.

3.  Draw a line that is 8 cm and another line below it that is 12 cm.

    Label the 8-cm line F and the 12-cm line G.
    Line F is _____ paper clips long.
    Line G is _____ paper clips long.
    Line G is _____ cm longer than Line F.
    Line F is _____ paper clips shorter than Line G.
    Lines F and G are _____ paper clips long.
    Lines F and G are _____ centimeters long.

**COMMON CORE**

Lesson 7:    Measure and compare lengths using standard metric length units
Date:        and non-standard lengths units; relate measurement to unit size.
             6/26/13

2.C.25

4. Line X is 1 meter. Line Y is 89 centimeters.

  Line X is _____ centimeters.

  Which line is longer?   Line X      Line Y         How much longer? _____cm

5. Line P is 2 meters. Line Q is 300 centimeters.

  Line P is _____ centimeters.

  Line Q is _____ meters.

  Which line is longer?   Line P      Line Q

  How much longer? _____

6. Jordan measured the length of a line with large paper clips. His friend measured the length of the same line with small paper clips.

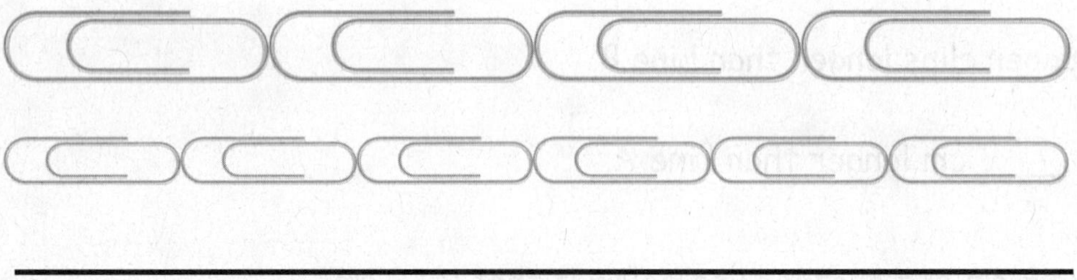

  About how many paper clips did Jordan use? _____ large paper clips.

  About how many small paper clips did his friend use? _____ small paper clips.

  Why did Jordan's friend need more paper clips to measure the same line as Jordan?

  _____

  _____

**COMMON CORE™**

**Lesson 7:**   Measure and compare lengths using standard metric length units
and non-standard lengths units; relate measurement to unit size.
**Date:**   6/26/13

2.C.26

## Topic D
# Relate Addition and Subtraction to Length

**2.MD.5, 2.MD.6,** 2.MD.1, 2.MD.3, 2.MD.4

| | | |
|---|---|---|
| **Focus Standard:** | 2.MD.5 | Use addition and subtraction within 100 to solve word problems involving lengths that are given in the same units, e.g., by using drawings (such as drawings of rulers) and equations with a symbol for the unknown number to represent the problem. |
| | 2.MD.6 | Represent whole numbers as lengths from 0 on a number line diagram with equally spaced points corresponding to the numbers 0, 1, 2, …, and represent whole-number sums and differences within 100 on a number line diagram. |
| **Instructional Days:** | 3 | |
| **Coherence   -Links from:** | GK–M3 | Comparison of Length, Weight, Capacity, and Numbers to 10 |
| | G1–M3 | Ordering and Comparing Length Measurements as Numbers |
| | G1–M6 | Place Value, Comparison, Addition and Subtraction to 100 |
| | G2–M7 | Problem Solving with Length, Money, and Data |
| **-Links to:** | G3–M2 | Place Value and Problem Solving With Units of Measure |
| | G3–M4 | Multiplication and Area |
| | G3–M7 | Geometry and Measurement Word Problems |

In Topic D, students relate addition and subtraction to length. They apply their conceptual understanding to choose appropriate tools and strategies (e.g., the ruler as a number line, benchmarks for estimation, tape diagrams for comparison) to solve word problems (**2.MD.5, 2.MD.6**).

In Topic A, students had their first experience creating and using a ruler as a number line. Now, students solve addition and subtraction word problems using the ruler as a number line. This concept is reinforced and practiced throughout the module in the fluency activities that involve using the meter strip for counting on and counting back, and is incorporated into the accompanying Problem Sets. Students then progress in the second lesson from concrete to abstract by creating tape diagrams to represent and compare lengths. The third lesson culminates with students solving two-step word problems involving measurement using like units.

**A Teaching Sequence Towards Mastery of Relating Addition and Subtraction to Length**

**Objective 1:** Solve addition and subtraction word problems using the ruler as a number line.
(Lesson 8)

**Objective 2:** Concrete to abstract: measure lengths of string using measurement tools; represent length with tape diagrams to represent and compare the lengths.
(Lesson 9)

**Objective 3:** Apply conceptual understanding of measurement by solving two-step word problems.
(Lesson 10)

# Lesson 8

Objective: Solve addition and subtraction word problems using the ruler as a number line.

## Suggested Lesson Structure

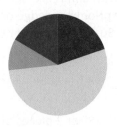

| | |
|---|---|
| ■ Fluency Practice | (12 minutes) |
| ■ Application Problems | (6 minutes) |
| ■ Concept Development | (32 minutes) |
| ■ Student Debrief | (10 minutes) |
| **Total Time** | **(60 minutes)** |

## Fluency Practice (12 minutes)

- How Many More to Make a Meter?  **2.MD.4**          (3 minutes)
- Making a Meter  **2.MD.4**          (9 minutes)

### How Many More to Make a Meter? (3 minutes)

T:   For every number of centimeters I say, you say the number needed to make a meter.  If I say 70 centimeters, you say 30 centimeters. Ready?

T:   70 centimeters.

S:   30 centimeters.

T:   Number sentence.

S:   70 cm + 30 cm = 1 m.

T:   40 centimeters.

S:   60 centimeters.

T:   Number sentence.

S:   40 cm + 60 cm = 1 m.

Continue with possible sequences: 20 cm, 90 cm, 10 cm, 9 cm, 11 cm, 50 cm, 49 cm, 51 cm

### Sprint:  Making a Meter (9 minutes)

Materials:  (S) Making a Meter Sprint

| Lesson 8: | Solve addition and subtraction word problems using the ruler as a number line. |
|---|---|
| Date: | 6/26/13 |

2.D.3

## Application Problem  (6 minutes)

For Valentine's Day, Suzie is mailing a painting to her Nana.  The painting is 16 centimeters long.  The gift box is 35 centimeters long.  How much longer is the gift box than the painting?  Draw a picture to show your work.

Extension:  What would happen if Suzie's meter strip was torn and started at 1 centimeter instead of zero?  Would she still be able to measure?  (Students orally defend their reasoning.)

Note:  The problem allows for practice of *compare with difference unknown* word problems.  The question sets the stage for today's objective as students use their prior knowledge of movement on a number line (meter strip) to defend their reasoning as they think about Suzie's torn meter strip.

## Concept Development  (32 minutes)

Materials:  (T) 1 piece large construction paper (12" x 18" or 2 pieces of 8 ½" x 11" sheets taped together), torn meter strip  (S) 1 meter strip per student torn or cut at different points (i.e., cut meter strip at 4 cm, 5 cm, or 1 cm), 1 piece of large construction paper per student, personal boards for each student

T:   I am throwing a party and want to decorate my house.  I will start with my front door and put some ribbon around its edges.  How can we figure out how long the ribbon should be?

S:   Figure out the length around the door using benchmarks like the height of the knob.  → Measure around the door with a meter stick and make the ribbon the same length.

T:   That is what I did. I used a meter stick to find the measurements.  (Draw the door and label each side. The top is 1 meters, left side is 2 meters, bottom is 1 meter, right side is 2 meters.)  How long does the ribbon need to be to go all the way around my door?  Share with a partner.

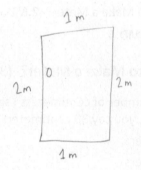

S:   6 m.  → I added all 4 sides and got 6 meters.  → I added 2 + 2 + 1 + 1 = 6.

T:   I also want to string lights up one side of the steps leading to my front door.  Help me figure out the length of the string of lights if they line the edges of the steps.

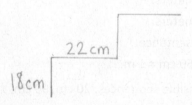

T:   There are 2 steps.  (Draw the diagram labeling only the stair 18 cm and 22 cm.)  How many centimeters of lights do I need to line the entire length of both steps?  Put your finger on 0.  Slide your finger up to 18 centimeters.

T:   How much more do we need to add?

T:   Now move up two.  We are at 20 centimeters.  How far should we move our finger on the meter strip?

Lesson 8:   Solve addition and subtraction word problems using the ruler as a
            number line.
Date:       6/26/13

2.D.4

S:   We should move it 20 centimeters.

T:   Where will our finger stop?

S:   At 40 centimeters.

T:   Where will we be on the meter strip when we add the
     second stair?  How do you know?

S:   We'll be at 80 centimeters, because you need to add
     18 + 22 again. → We'll be at 80 centimeters.  You just
     have to double 40 centimeters.

T:   I have a string of lights that is 1 meter long.  Is it long
     enough to reach the top of the steps?

    S:   Yes, because a meter is longer than 80
     centimeters. → Yes, because 1 meter is 100
     centimeters and you only need 80 centimeters. →
     100 cm – 80 cm = 20 cm left over.

T:   Let's suppose that I taped the meter strip directly
     onto the steps, with 0 at the bottom, to measure the
     length of the string of lights needed to reach the top.
     This time I decide to start the lights after the first 18
     centimeters, but I don't want to move the meter strip.
     How can I determine how long the string of lights
     should be now?

S:   You can pretend that the 18 is 0 and count up 2 to 20, then count up by 10s to reach 80.  You would
     need 62 centimeters of lights. → You can subtract 80 – 18 to get 62 centimeters.

T:   I also want to hang a party sign with this piece of string, I want to know the length of the string, but I
     tore my meter strip, and now it starts at 4 centimeters.  (show students model of torn meter strip).
     How can I still use this torn strip to measure my piece of string?

S:   Use it the same as usual.  Start at the beginning of the meter strip and measure. → Count the number
     of centimeters. → We can start at 4 centimeters on our meter strip and subtract 4 from where the
     string ends on the meter strip.

T:   Watch me as I line up the string with the torn meter strip.  Where does the string end?

**MP.2**   S:   At 29 centimeters.

T:   Now let's take away 4 cm from 29 centimeters.  What is the length of the string?

S:   The string is 25 centimeters.

T:   I ordered a cake and I want to make sure it will fit on the table.  The cake is the same size as this piece
     of construction paper.  The table is the same size as your desks.  Can you figure out the length of the
     cake and the desk?

T:   I have torn meter strips for you to measure with.  With your partner, measure the length of the cake
     and desk.  Record your answers on your personal white boards.

Students measure and return to the carpet to share their answers.

    T:   What strategy did you and your partner use to measure the lengths with the torn meter strip?

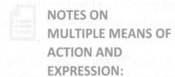

**NOTES ON
MULTIPLE MEANS OF
ACTION AND
EXPRESSION:**

Get students up and moving by
using a number line floor mat to
illustrate the idea of moving the
zero point.

- Invite a student to begin at 4
  and jump 25 length units.
  Students can count on chorally,
  starting at 4.  Encourage them to
  add 1 to make 5; then, count up
  by 10s.

- Teacher asks:  Do you notice a
  relationship between 0, 4, 25,
  29?

Lesson 8:    Solve addition and subtraction word problems using the ruler as a
                  number line.

Date:    6/26/13

2.D.5

S:    We started at the beginning of our meter strip and counted on. → We lined up the meter strip with the lengths and subtracted 4 centimeters from where the object stopped.

T:    What is the difference between the length of the table and the length of the cake? (For this example, assume the cake is 45 centimeters and the desk is 60 centimeters.)

S:    60 cm – 45 cm is 15 cm. → 45 cm + 15 more cm = 60 cm.

T:    So we know it is long enough. Let's repeat the process to see if it is wide enough for the cake.

If necessary repeat the process above with a few more examples:

- Students measure an envelope and an invitation (index card) to see if the envelopes are the right size.

- Students measure 80 centimeters of streamer to see if it will fit across the width of the door, the width of the door being about a meter.

Otherwise, invite students to begin the Problem Set.

**NOTES ON MULTIPLE MEANS OF REPRESENTATION:**

Invite students to come forward and model differing solution methods for Problem 5(c) on the chalkboard.

Did anyone arrive at the same solution but in a different way? Can you explain how you solved it?

What would happen if I subtracted 7 meters from 5 meters? Could I subtract first and *then* add?

## Problem Set (10 minutes)

Students should do their personal best to complete the Problem Set within the allotted 10 minutes. For some classes, it may be appropriate to modify the assignment by specifying which problems they work on first. Some problems do not specify a method for solving. Students solve these problems using the RDW approach used for Application Problems.

## Student Debrief (10 minutes)

**Lesson Objective**: Solve addition and subtraction word problems using the ruler as a **number line**.

The Student Debrief is intended to invite reflection and active processing of the total lesson experience.

Invite students to review their solutions for the Problem Set. They should check work by comparing answers with a partner before going over answers as a class. Look for misconceptions or misunderstandings that can be

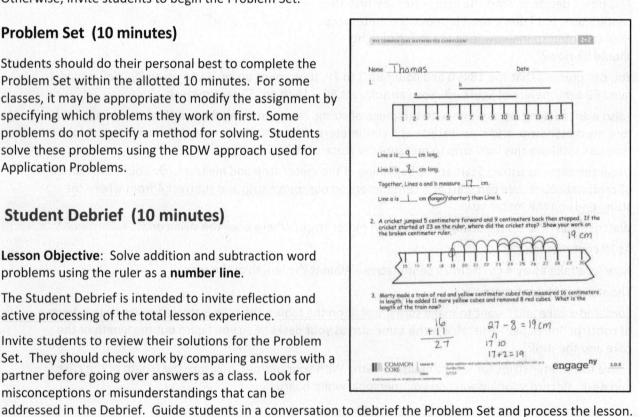

addressed in the Debrief. Guide students in a conversation to debrief the Problem Set and process the lesson.

You may choose to use any combination of the questions below to lead the discussion.

MP.2

- Explain to your partner how you solved Problem 1. What similarities or differences were there in your solution methods?

- What strategies did you use to solve Problem 2 and Problem 3? Invite students to compare their drawings for Problem 3.

- How can you solve a problem with a ruler that doesn't start at zero?

- How is a ruler similar to a **number line**?

- Look at Problem 5. What math strategies did you need to know in order to solve this problem? (Students might answer counting on, skip counting, adding, and subtracting.)

- How did we use addition and subtraction today?

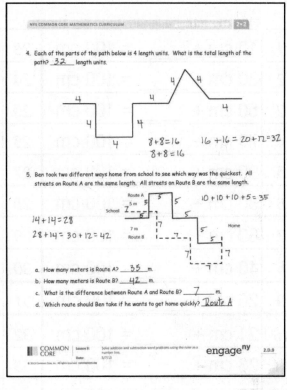

## Exit Ticket (3 minutes)

After the Student Debrief, instruct students to complete the Exit Ticket. A review of their work will help you assess the students' understanding of the concepts that were presented in the lesson today and plan more effectively for future lessons. You may read the questions aloud to the students.

# A

**# Correct** _____

Find the missing length to make 1 meter.

| | | | | |
|---|---|---|---|---|
| 1 | 10 cm + _____ = 100 cm | 23 | _____ + 62 cm = 1 m |
| 2 | 30 cm + _____ = 100 cm | 24 | _____ + 72 cm = 1 m |
| 3 | 50 cm + _____ = 100 cm | 25 | _____ + 92 cm = 1 m |
| 4 | 70 cm + _____ = 100 cm | 26 | _____ + 29 cm = 1 m |
| 5 | 90 cm + _____ = 100 cm | 27 | _____ + 39 cm = 1 m |
| 6 | 80 cm + _____ = 100 cm | 28 | _____ + 59 cm = 1 m |
| 7 | 60 cm + _____ = 100 cm | 29 | _____ + 89 cm = 1 m |
| 8 | 40 cm + _____ = 100 cm | 30 | _____ + 88 cm = 1 m |
| 9 | 20 cm + _____ = 100 cm | 31 | _____ + 68 cm = 1 m |
| 10 | 21 cm + _____ = 100 cm | 32 | _____ + 18 cm = 1 m |
| 11 | 23 cm + _____ = 100 cm | 33 | _____ + 15 cm = 1 m |
| 12 | 25 cm + _____ = 100 cm | 34 | _____ + 55 cm = 1 m |
| 13 | 27 cm + _____ = 100 cm | 35 | 44 cm + _____ = 1 m |
| 14 | 37 cm + _____ = 100 cm | 36 | 55 cm + _____ = 1 m |
| 15 | 38 cm + _____ = 100 cm | 37 | 88 cm + _____ = 1 m |
| 16 | 39 cm + _____ = 100 cm | 38 | 1 m = _____ + 33 cm |
| 17 | 49 cm + _____ = 100 cm | 39 | 1 m = _____ + 66 cm |
| 18 | 50 cm + _____ = 100 cm | 40 | 1 m = _____ + 99 cm |
| 19 | 52 cm + _____ = 100 cm | 41 | 1 m - 11 cm = _____ |
| 20 | 56 cm + _____ = 100 cm | 42 | 1 m - 15 cm = _____ |
| 21 | 58 cm + _____ = 100 cm | 43 | 1 m - 17 cm = _____ |
| 22 | 62 cm + _____ = 100 cm | 44 | 1 m - 19 cm = _____ |

**COMMON CORE**        **Lesson 8:**    Solve addition and subtraction word problems using the ruler as a
                                  number line.                                                          2.D.8
                    **Date:**      6/26/13

# B

# Correct _____

Find the missing length to make 1 meter.

| | | | | | |
|---|---|---|---|---|---|
| 1 | 1 cm + _____ = 100 cm | 23 | _____ + 72 cm = 1 m |
| 2 | 10 cm + _____ = 100 cm | 24 | _____ + 82 cm = 1 m |
| 3 | 20 cm + _____ = 100 cm | 25 | _____ + 28 cm = 1 m |
| 4 | 40 cm + _____ = 100 cm | 26 | _____ + 38 cm = 1 m |
| 5 | 60 cm + _____ = 100 cm | 27 | _____ + 48 cm = 1 m |
| 6 | 80 cm + _____ = 100 cm | 28 | _____ + 45 cm = 1 m |
| 7 | 90 cm + _____ = 100 cm | 29 | _____ + 43 cm = 1 m |
| 8 | 70 cm + _____ = 100 cm | 30 | _____ + 34 cm = 1 m |
| 9 | 50 cm + _____ = 100 cm | 31 | _____ + 24 cm = 1 m |
| 10 | 30 cm + _____ = 100 cm | 32 | _____ + 14 cm = 1 m |
| 11 | 31 cm + _____ = 100 cm | 33 | _____ + 12 cm = 1 m |
| 12 | 33 cm + _____ = 100 cm | 34 | _____ + 10 cm = 1 m |
| 13 | 35 cm + _____ = 100 cm | 35 | 11 cm + _____ = 1m |
| 14 | 37 cm + _____ = 100 cm | 36 | 33 cm + _____ = 1 m |
| 15 | 39 cm + _____ = 100 cm | 37 | 55 cm + _____ = 1 m |
| 16 | 49 cm + _____ = 100 cm | 38 | 1 m = _____ + 22 cm |
| 17 | 59 cm + _____ = 100 cm | 39 | 1 m = _____ + 88 cm |
| 18 | 60 cm + _____ = 100 cm | 40 | 1 m = _____ + 99 cm |
| 19 | 62 cm + _____ = 100 cm | 41 | 1 m - 1 cm = _____ |
| 20 | 66 cm + _____ = 100 cm | 42 | 1 m - 5 cm = _____ |
| 21 | 68 cm + _____ = 100 cm | 43 | 1 m - 7 cm = _____ |
| 22 | 72 cm + _____ = 100 cm | 44 | 1 m - 17 cm = _____ |

**COMMON CORE™** Lesson 8: Solve addition and subtraction word problems using the ruler as a number line. 2.D.9

Date: 6/26/13

Name _____     Date _____

1.

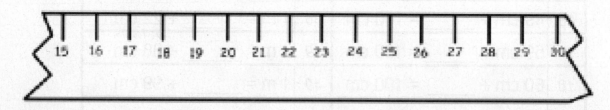

Line a is _____ cm long.

Line b is _____ cm long.

Together, Lines a and b measure _____ cm.

Line a is _____ cm (longer/shorter) than Line b.

2. A cricket jumped 5 centimeters forward and 9 centimeters back then stopped. If the cricket started at 23 on the ruler, where did the cricket stop? Show your work on the broken centimeter ruler.

3. Marty made a train of red and yellow centimeter cubes that measured 16 centimeters in length. He added 11 more yellow cubes and removed 8 red cubes. What is the length of the train now?

**COMMON CORE**

**Lesson 8:**   Solve addition and subtraction word problems using the ruler as a number line.

**Date:**   6/26/13

2.D.10

4. Each of the parts of the path below is 4 length units. What is the total length of the path? _____ length units.

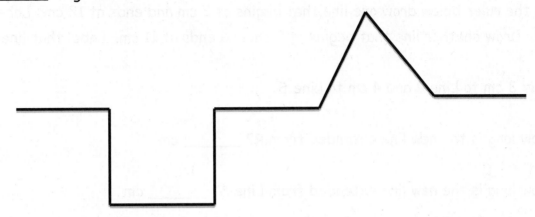

5. Ben took two different ways home from school to see which way was the quickest. All streets on Route A are the same length. All streets on Route B are the same length.

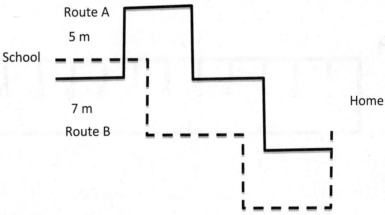

Route A

5 m

School

7 m

Route B

Home

a. How many meters is Route A? _____m.

b. How many meters is Route B? _____ m.

c. What is the difference between Route A and Route B? _____ m.

d. Which route should Ben take if he wants to get home quickly? _____

**COMMON CORE**

Lesson 8:     Solve addition and subtraction word problems using the ruler as a
              number line.
Date:         6/26/13

2.D.11

Name _____     Date _____

1. Using the ruler below draw one line that begins at 2 cm and ends at 12 cm.  Label that line R.  Draw another line that begins at 5 cm and ends at 11 cm.  Label that line S.

   a.  Add 3 cm to Line R and 4 cm to Line S.

   b.  How long is the new line extended from R? _____ cm

   c.  How long is the new line extended from Line S? _____ cm

   d.  The new line extended from Line S is _____ cm (shorter/longer) than the new line extended from Line R.

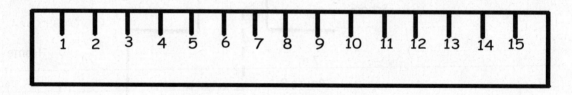

**COMMON CORE**

Lesson 8:     Solve addition and subtraction word problems using the ruler as a
Date:          number line.

6/26/13

2.D.12

© 2013 Common Core, Inc. All rights reserved. commoncore.org

Name _____     Date _____

1.  Line c is _____ cm.

    Line d is _____ cm.

    Lines c and d are _____ cm.

    Line c is _____ cm (longer/shorter) than Line d.

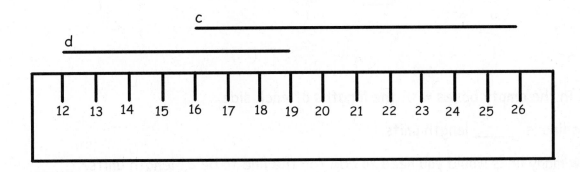

2.  A cardinal flew 12 meters north and then turned around and flew 5 meters south.  His starting point is marked on the ruler.  Where did is the cardinal now?  Show your work on the broken ruler.

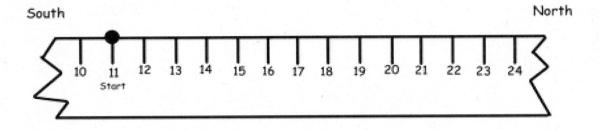

COMMON
CORE™

Lesson 8:    Solve addition and subtraction word problems using the ruler as a
              number line.
Date:        6/26/13

2.D.13

3. All of the sides of the line below are equal length units.

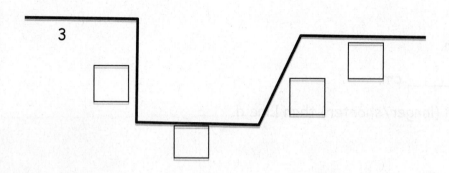

a. Fill in the empty boxes with the lengths of each side.

b. The line is _____ length units.

c. How many lines would you need to add for the line to be 21 length units? _____ lines

4. The length of a picture is 67 centimeters. The width of the picture is 48 centimeters. How many more centimeters is the length than the width?

# Lesson 9

Objective:  Concrete to abstract:  measure lengths of string using measurement tools; represent length with tape diagrams to represent and compare the lengths.

## Suggested Lesson Structure

■ Fluency Practice            (10 minutes)
■ Application Problems         (6 minutes)
■ Concept Development         (34 minutes)
■ Student Debrief             (10 minutes)
   **Total Time**             **(60 minutes)**

## Fluency Practice  (10 minutes)

▪ Adding Multiples of 10 to Numbers  **2.NBT.5**          (6 minutes)
▪ Happy Counting by Centimeters  **2.NBT.2**              (4 minutes)

### Meter Strip Addition:  Adding Multiples of 10 to Numbers  (6 minutes)

Materials:  (S) Meter strips (as pictured)

Note:  Students apply knowledge of using the ruler as a number line to fluently add multiples of ten.  The meter strip solidifies the process for visual and tactile learners, and creates the groundwork for students to make tape diagrams in the lesson.

T:  (Each student has a meter strip.)  Put your finger on 0 to start.  I'll say the whole measurement.  Slide up to that number.  Add 10 centimeters and tell me how many centimeters your finger is from 0.

T:  Let's try one.  Fingers at 0 centimeters!  (Pause)  30 centimeters.

S:  (Students slide their fingers to 30.)

T:  Remember to add 10.  (Pause.)  How far is your finger from 0?

S:  40 centimeters.

Continue with the following possible sequence:  45 cm, 51 cm, 63 cm, 76 cm, 87 cm, and 98 cm.  As your students show mastery, advance to adding 20 centimeters.

Lesson 9:    Concrete to abstract:  measure the lengths of string using measurement tools; represent length with tape diagrams to represent and compare the lengths.
Date:        6/26/13

2.D.15

## Happy Counting by Centimeters  (4 minutes)

Note:  Students practice counting by 10 centimeters and exchanging centimeters for meters.  This activity relates to Say Ten counting, where ones are exchanged for tens.  It can be demonstrated on a Rekenrek, with each bead representing 10 centimeters.

T:  Let's count by 10 centimeters, starting at 80 centimeters.  When we get to 100 centimeters, we say 1 meter and then we will count by meters and centimeters.  Ready?  (Rhythmically point up until a change is desired.  Show a closed hand then point down.  Continue, mixing it up.)

S:  80 cm, 90 cm, 1m, 1m 10 cm, 1 m 20 cm, 1 m 30 cm, 1 m 40 cm, 1m 50 cm (stop) 1 m 40 cm, 1 m 30 cm, 1 m 20 cm (stop) 1 m 30 cm, 1 m 40 cm, 1 m 50 cm, 1 m 60 cm, 1 m 70 cm, 1 m 80 cm, 1 m 90 cm, 2 m, 1 m 90 cm, 2 m, 2 m 10 cm, 2 m 20 cm, 2 m 10 cm, 2 m, 1 m 90 cm, etc.

T:  Excellent!  Try it for 30 seconds with your partner starting at 80 centimeters.  Partner B, you are the teacher today.

## Application Problem  (6 minutes)

Mei's frog leaped several centimeters.  Then it leaped 34 centimeters.  In all, it leaped 50 centimeters.  How far did Mei's frog leap at first?  Draw a picture and write a number sentence to explain your thinking.

Note:  This *add to with start unknown* situation may be challenging for students.  After students share their solutions, the teacher may wish to model problem solving using a tape diagram.  This is in anticipation of today's lesson, where students will be representing length using tape diagrams.

## Concept Development  (34 minutes)

Materials:  (T) 2 lengths of string in 2 different colors (3 meters red and 5 meters blue), meter stick  (S) 1 meter tape and 50-cm piece of string per pair of students, masking tape

T:  (Use masking tape to make two lines on the floor before class begins.  Make one line squiggly, that measures 3 meters, and one line zigzag that measures 5 meters.  Convene students on the carpet, perhaps seated in a U-shape.)

T:  Make an estimate, how long is the zigzag line?

S:  (Students share estimates.)

T:  Make an estimate, how long is the squiggly line?

S:  (Students share estimates.)

T:  Which line do you think is longer?

**NOTES ON MULTIPLE MEANS OF ENGAGEMENT:**

To support ELLs, treat the student's first language as a resource.  When drawing tape diagrams, students need to understand comparative language in order to represent and compare various lengths.  The teacher can use the student's first language to foster understanding.  For example,

- In Spanish, shorter = *mas corto*.
- In Spanish, longer = *mas largo*.

Lesson 9:   Concrete to abstract:  measure the lengths of string using measurement tools; represent length with tape diagrams to represent and compare the lengths.

Date:   6/26/13

2.D.16

S:   We don't know because they aren't straight. → The squiggly line because it starts at the wall and goes past the rug. The other line starts at the wall and doesn't reach the rug. → You need to measure both to know.

T:   How can I find out the actual length of each line to check our estimates?

S:   Measure each part and add them together. → Measure each part and count on as you go.

T:   That may work for the zigzag line, but that won't work for the squiggly line.

T:   I have some string here. How do you think this string could help me measure both lines?

S:   Take the string and trace it along the line. → Hold it down with one hand and lay it down along the tape.

T:   (Use the red string to measure the squiggly line and the blue string to measure the zigzag line.)

T:   Now, how can I compare the lengths of the lines?

S:   Measure the strings.

T:   These strings are very long. Let's tape them on the floor and see how long they are.

T:   (Lay the red and blue strings parallel on the floor and horizontal to the students.)

T:   Use a benchmark to estimate the length of each string. Share your estimates with your neighbor.

T:   What measurement tool could we use to check the estimates?

S:   A meter tape. → A meter stick. (Call two volunteers to measure.)

S:   The red string is 3 meters. The blue string is 5 meters.

T:   I don't have enough space on the board to tape these long strings. What could I do instead?

S:   Draw a picture. → Write the numbers.

T:   (Draw a horizontal rectangular bar to represent the length of the red string.) This represents the red string. Tell me when to stop to show the blue string. (Start at the left end of the red bar and move to the right, making a second bar underneath the first.)

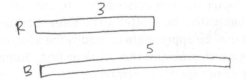

S:   Stop!

T:   Why should I stop here?

S:   Because the second bar should be longer than the first bar.

MP.5

T:   Let's write the measurements of each string above.

T:   (Label both bars.) What number sentence could you use to describe the total length of these strings?

S:   3 + 5 = ☐

T:   What number sentence could I use to describe the difference in length between these two strings?

S:   5 − 3 = ☐

T:   This is called a tape diagram. It is helpful because I can draw a small picture to represent any length.

T:   Let's practice making a tape diagram.

T:   What is the measurement around my wrist? (Demonstrate wrapping the string around your wrist and pinching the end point, then lay the string along a meter stick to determine the length.)S:   16 centimeters.

T:   Let's compare the length around my wrist to the length around my head. What's the length around my

| Lesson 9: | Concrete to abstract: measure the lengths of string using measurement tools; represent length with tape diagrams to represent and compare the lengths. | 2.D.17 |
| Date: | 6/26/13 | |

© 2013 Common Core, Inc. All rights reserved. **commoncore.org**

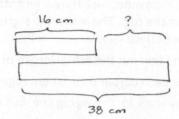

head? (Repeat the demonstration process and record the length on the board.)

S:   38 centimeters.

T:   Draw along with me as I draw the first bar on the board to represent my wrist measurement. We'll label this 16 centimeters. (Students draw.)

**MP.5**

T:   Right below that, draw the second bar to show my head measurement. Should the bar be longer or shorter?

S:   Longer. (Students draw and label the second bar 38 centimeters.)

T:   Look at your diagram. Talk with your neighbor: What is this open space between the end of the first and second bars?

S:   It's how much longer 38 centimeters is than 16 centimeters. → It's the difference between 16 centimeters and 38 centimeters. → It's the difference between the measurement of your wrist and your head.

T:   What number sentences can we use to find the difference between 16 centimeters and 38 centimeters?

S:   38 – 16 = ☐ → 16 + ☐ = 38.

Check students' tape diagrams. Have them compare next the measurement around their thigh and the length of their arm, the length around their neck, and the length around their head.

## Problem Set  (10 minutes)

Students should do their personal best to complete the Problem Set within the allotted 10 minutes. For some classes, it may be appropriate to modify the assignment by specifying which problems they work on first. Some problems do not specify a method for solving. Students solve these problems using the RDW approach used for Application Problems.

## Student Debrief  (10 minutes)

**Lesson Objective:** Measure lengths of string and use tape diagrams to represent and compare lengths.

The Student Debrief is intended to invite reflection and active processing of the total lesson experience.

Invite students to review their solutions for the Problem Set. They should check work by comparing answers with a partner before going over answers as a class. Look for

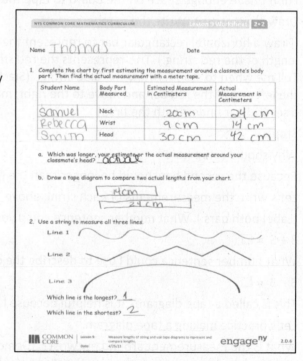

misconceptions or misunderstandings that can be addressed in the Debrief. Guide students in a conversation to debrief the Problem Set and process the lesson. You may choose to use any combination of the questions below to lead the discussion.

Lesson 9:   Concrete to abstract: measure the lengths of string using measurement tools; represent length with tape diagrams to represent and compare the lengths.
Date:       6/26/13

2.D.18

- What estimation strategies did you use for Problem 1? How were they similar to or different from your partner's strategies? (Teacher charts benchmark strategies).

- Look at Problems 2 and 3. What steps did you take to draw an accurate tape diagram? How do your drawings compare to your partner's?

- Add to the application problem: Anthony's frog leaped 28 centimeters. With a partner, students draw a tape diagram to compare the distances that the two frogs leapt. Teacher samples tape diagrams: What does this part represent in your solution number sentence?

- How did you show your thinking today?

**MP.5**

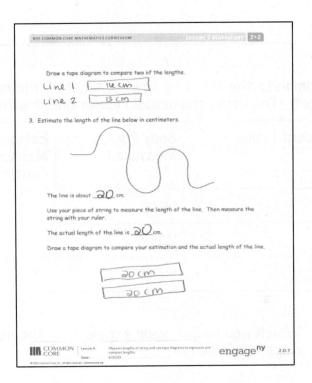

## Exit Ticket (3 minutes)

After the Student Debrief, instruct students to complete the Exit Ticket. A review of their work will help you assess the students' understanding of the concepts that were presented in the lesson today and plan more effectively for future lessons. You may read the questions aloud to the students.

**NOTES ON MULTIPLE MEANS OF ACTION AND EXPRESSION:**

As students return to the application problem, adjust the difficulty level of the extension:

Choose challenging problem types, such as , "How would your tape diagram change if Mei's frog leaped $x$ centimeters more than Anthony's?"

Invite students to write their own comparison word problem with an accompanying tape diagram.

Lesson 9:   Concrete to abstract:  measure the lengths of string using measurement tools; represent length with tape diagrams to represent and compare the lengths.

Date:   6/26/13

2.D.19

© 2013 Common Core, Inc. All rights reserved. commoncore.org

Name _____   Date _____

1. Complete the chart by first estimating the measurement around a classmate's body part. Then find the actual measurement with a meter tape.

| Student Name | Body Part Measured | Estimated Measurement in Centimeters | Actual Measurement in Centimeters |
| --- | --- | --- | --- |
| | Neck | | |
| | Wrist | | |
| | Head | | |

   a. Which was longer, your estimate or the actual measurement around your classmate's head? _____

   b. Draw a tape diagram to compare two actual lengths from your chart.

2. Use a string to measure all three lines.

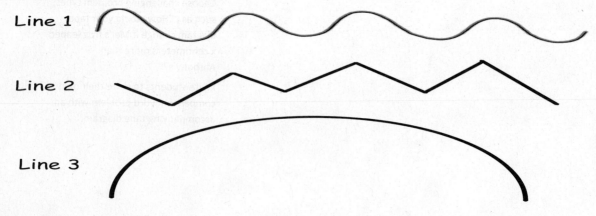

Line 1

Line 2

Line 3

   Which line is the longest? _____

COMMON CORE

Lesson 9:    Concrete to abstract: measure the lengths of string using measurement tools; represent length with tape diagrams to represent and compare the lengths.

Date:       6/26/13

2.D.20

Which line in the shortest? _____

Draw a tape diagram to compare two of the lengths.

3. Estimate the length of the line below in centimeters.

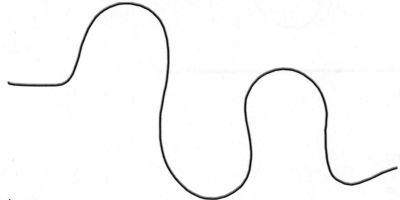

The line is about _____ cm.

Use your piece of string to measure the length of the line. Then measure the string with your ruler.

The actual length of the line is _____cm.

Draw a tape diagram to compare your estimation and the actual length of the line.

**COMMON CORE™**

**Lesson 9:** Concrete to abstract: measure the lengths of string using measurement tools; represent length with tape diagrams to represent and compare the lengths.

**Date:** 6/26/13

2.D.21

Name _____    Date _____

1. Measure the two lines by using your string.  Write the length in centimeters.

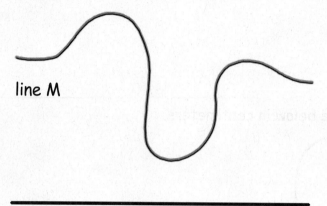

line M

line N

Line M is _____ cm long.

Line N is _____ cm long.

2. Mandy measured the lines and said both lines are the same length.
   Is Mandy's answer correct?  Yes or no.  _____

   Explain why or why not.

   _____

   _____

3. Draw a tape diagram to compare the two lengths.

**COMMON CORE™**    Lesson 9:    Concrete to abstract:  measure the lengths of string using
measurement tools; represent length with tape diagrams to
represent and compare the lengths.

2.D.22

Date:    6/26/13

Name _____    Date _____

1. Find the measurement around three round objects in your house.  Complete the chart below.

| Object Name | Estimated Measurement in Centimeters | Actual Measurement in Centimeters |
|---|---|---|
|  |  |  |
|  |  |  |
|  |  |  |

a. What is the difference between the greatest and shortest measurements?
_____cm.

b. Draw a tape diagram comparing the estimated measurements.

c. Draw a tape diagram to compare the actual measurements.

**COMMON CORE**™    Lesson 9:    Concrete to abstract:  measure the lengths of string using measurement tools; represent length with tape diagrams to represent and compare the lengths.    **2.D.23**

Date:    6/26/13

2. Measure the two lines below.

line A

line B

a. Line A is ____cm.

b. Line B is ____ cm.

c. Together, lines A and B measure _____ cm.

d. Line A is _____cm (shorter/longer) than line B.

3. Kim is decorating a table for a party.  Measure the ribbon she is using to decorate.

The ribbon is _____ cm long.

Kim needs 1 meter of ribbon.

How much more ribbon does Kim need than what she has? _____cm.

**COMMON CORE™**

**Lesson 9:**    Concrete to abstract:  measure the lengths of string using
measurement tools; represent length with tape diagrams to
represent and compare the lengths.
**Date:**    6/26/13

2.D.24

4. Shawn and Steven had a contest to see who could jump the furthest.  Shawn jumped 75 centimeters.  Steven jumped 23 more centimeters than Shawn.

a. How far did Steven jump? _____ centimeters

b. How won the jumping contest? _____

c. Draw a tape diagram to compare the lengths that Shawn and Steven jumped.

Lesson 9:

Date:

Concrete to abstract:  measure the lengths of string using measurement tools; represent length with tape diagrams to represent and compare the lengths.

6/26/13

2.D.25

# Lesson 10

Objective: Apply conceptual understanding of measurement by solving two-step word problems.

## Suggested Lesson Structure

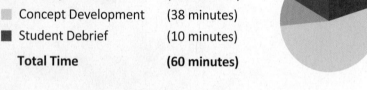

- Fluency Practice        (12 minutes)
- Concept Development      (38 minutes)
- Student Debrief         (10 minutes)
- **Total Time**          **(60 minutes)**

## Fluency Practice  (12 minutes)

- Subtracting Multiples of 10 from Numbers  **2.NBT.5**      (6 minutes)
- Take From Ten  **2.OA.2**      (3 minutes)
- Relate Subtraction to Addition  **2.OA.2**      (3 minutes)

### Meter Strip Subtraction:  Subtracting Multiples of 10 from Numbers  (6 minutes)

Materials:  (S) Meter strips (as pictured)

Note:  Students fluently subtract multiples of ten while using the ruler as a number line.

- T:  Put your finger on 0 to start.  I'll say the whole measurement.  Slide up to that number.  Then take away 10 centimeters and tell me how many centimeters your finger is from 0.
- T:  Fingers at 0 centimeters! (Pause.)  30 centimeters.
- S:  (Students slide their fingers to 30.)
- T:  Remember to take 10.  (Pause.)  How far is your finger from 0?
- S:  20 centimeters.

Continue with the following possible sequence:  45cm, 52cm, 64cm, 74cm, 82cm, 91cm, 99 cm.  Repeat the sequence but sliding back 20.

**COMMON CORE**

Lesson 10:   Apply conceptual understanding of measurement by solving two-step word problems.
Date:   6/26/13

2.D.26

## Take From Ten  (3 minutes)

Note:  Students revisit this activity from Module 1 in preparation for more practice of subtraction in Module 3.
Draw a number bond for the first example to model student thinking to solve.

**(Draw on board)**
**12 − 3 =**

  /\

 **2  1**

T:  For every number sentence I say, you will give a subtraction
number sentence that takes from the ten first.  When I say
12 - 3, you say 12 − 2 − 1.  Ready?

T:  12 − 3.

S:  12 − 2 − 1.

T:  Answer.

S:  9.

Continue with the possible sequences:   $12 - 4$, $12 - 5$, $14 - 5$, $14 - 6$, $14 - 7$, $15 - 7$, $15 - 8$, $15 - 9$, $16 - 9$, and
$16 - 8$.

## Relate Subtraction to Addition  (3 minutes)

Note:  The review of Module 1 activity challenges students to mentally subtract the ones and add the
difference to 10.  Draw a number bond for the first example to support student answers.  (Students may
answer verbally or on their personal boards.)

T:  2 − 1.

S:  1.

T:  When I say 12 − 1, you say 10 + 1. Ready?  12 − 1.

S:  10 + 1.

T:  3 − 1.

S:  2.

T:  13 − 1.

S:  10 + 2.

T:  Answer.

S:  12.

Continue with possible sequences: $14 - 1$, $15 - 1$, $16 - 1$, $17 - 1$, $17 -
2$, $17 - 4$, $16 - 4$, $15 - 4$, $15 - 2$, and $14 - 2$.

> **NOTES ON
> MULTIPLE MEANS OF
> REPRESENTATION:**
>
> Students who are struggling with
> pictorial representations may need
> to use concrete models (e.g., base
> ten blocks) to demonstrate
> conceptual understanding of
> addition and subtraction.  The
> teacher can also add incremented
> bars to the tape diagram as a
> transition from base ten blocks to a
> pictorial model.

## Concept Development  (38 minutes)

Materials:  (S) Personal white boards

Post the 2 problems on the board.  Under each problem make two sections labeled Step 1 and Step 2.  Cover
the second problem until that portion of the lesson.

Lesson 10:     Apply conceptual understanding of measurement by solving two-
                 step word problems.

Date:        6/26/13

**Problem 1**

Mr. Peterson decorated 15 meters of ribbon in the morning.  He decorated 8 more meters in the afternoon than in the morning.  How many meters did Mr. Peterson decorate in the morning and afternoon in all?

T:   Let's read Problem 1 together.  (Read number one chorally.)

T:   (Draw a bar on the board under Step 1 and label it morning.)

T:   How many meters did Mr. Peterson decorate in the morning?

S:   15 meters.

T:   When did he decorate again?

S:   In the afternoon.

T:   Did he decorate more or less meters in the afternoon?

S:   More!

T:   How many more meters?

S:   8 more meters.

T:   Tell me when to stop drawing.  (Start to draw a second bar under the first bar to represent the afternoon meters.)

S:   Stop!

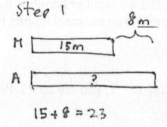

T:   What is this measurement here, the difference between his ribbon in the morning and afternoon?

S:   8 meters.

T:   And what is this length?  (Point to the part of the bar directly below the morning measurement.)

S:   15 meters.

T:   (Draw a line to separate that part and label the question mark below.)

T:   What is the length of the ribbon Mr. Peterson decorated in the afternoon?

S:   23 meters.

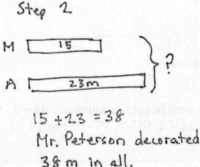

T:   What do we still need to find out?

S:   Figure out how many meters in the morning AND in the afternoon. → Add the morning meters and the afternoon meters.

T:   This is Step 2.  (Redraw the same model with the 23 meters recorded and the question mark to the right as shown to the right.)

T:   How many meters in the morning and afternoon did Mr. Peterson decorate?  Turn and talk.

S:   38 because 15 and 23 makes 38. → 10 + 20 = 30 and 5 + 3 = 8, 30 + 8 = 38.

T:   (Cross out the question mark and write 38 to show the solution.)  You just solved Step 2.

Lesson 10:     Apply conceptual understanding of measurement by solving two-
Date:          step word problems.
               6/26/13

## Problem 2

The red colored pencil is 17 centimeters long. The green colored pencil is 9 centimeters shorter than the red colored pencil. What is the total length of both pencils?

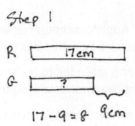

Lead the students through a similar process to that of Problem 1. Have them work the problem with you.

Step 1: Model and label the length of the red pencil, the difference in the lengths of the pencils and the question mark. Find the length of the green pencil. Write your number sentence.

Step 2: Redraw the model with 8 centimeters labeled into the lower bar and the unknown marked to the right with a question mark and bracket. Find the total of both lengths. Write your number sentence and statement of the solution.

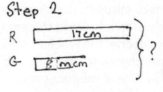

Once having completed both problems, have students compare Problems 1 and 2.

## Problem Set  (10 minutes)

Students should do their personal best to complete the Problem Set within the allotted 10 minutes. For some classes, it may be appropriate to modify the assignment by specifying which problems they work on first. Some problems do not specify a method for solving. Students solve these problems using the RDW approach used for Application Problems.

**NOTES ON
MULTIPLE MEANS OF
ENGAGEMENT:**

While students are completing the Problem Set, check frequently for understanding by saying, "Show me," with concrete models or tape diagrams. Modify two-step word problems so that they only involve single-digit addends. Assign struggling students to a buddy to clarify processes.

Lesson 10:      Apply conceptual understanding of measurement by solving two-
                step word problems.
Date:           6/26/13

2.D.29

## Student Debrief  (10 minutes)

**Lesson Objective**:  Apply conceptual understanding of measurement by solving two-step word problems.

The Student Debrief is intended to invite reflection and active processing of the total lesson experience.

Invite students to review their solutions for the Problem Set.  They should check work by comparing answers with a partner before going over answers as a class.  Look for misconceptions or misunderstandings that can be addressed in the Debrief.  Guide students in a conversation to debrief the Problem Set and process the lesson.  You may choose to use any combination of the questions below to lead the discussion.

**MP.3**

- How was your drawing for Problem 2, Step 1, similar to the model drawn for Problem 1, Step 1?

- With your partner, compare your tape diagrams for Problem 2, Step 2.  How did you label them?  Where did you place your addends?  How did you show the change (smaller, taller)?  Where did you draw brackets?

- Look at Problem 3.  How did you change your tape diagram in Step 2 to find the total length of the leather strips?

- What must you do when drawing tape diagrams and comparing lengths in order to be accurate?

- How could we arrive at the same answer to today's problems but in a different way?  What other math strategies can you connect with this (e.g., part–whole, number bond figures)?

- How do tape diagrams help you to solve problems with more than one step?

## Exit Ticket  (3 minutes)

After the Student Debrief, instruct students to complete the Exit Ticket.  A review of their work will help you assess the students' understanding of the concepts that were presented in the lesson today and plan more effectively for future lessons.  You may read the questions aloud to the students.

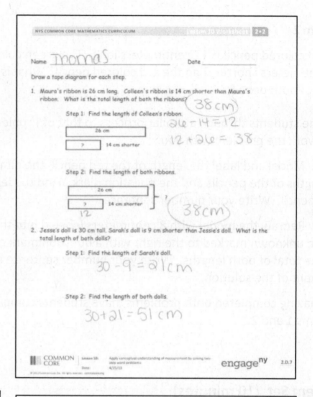

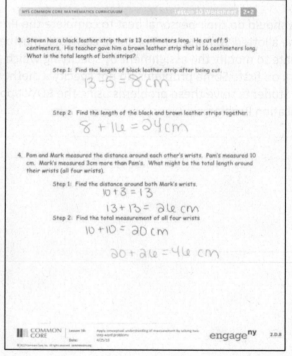

**COMMON CORE**

Lesson 10:     Apply conceptual understanding of measurement by solving two-
                     step word problems.
Date:            6/26/13

2.D.30

# A

Subtract.

# Correct _____

| | | | | | |
|---|---|---|---|---|---|
| 1 | 53 - 2 = | | 23 | 84 - 40 = | |
| 2 | 65 - 3 = | | 24 | 80 - 50 = | |
| 3 | 77 - 4 = | | 25 | 86 - 50 = | |
| 4 | 89 - 5 = | | 26 | 70 - 60 = | |
| 5 | 99 - 6 = | | 27 | 77 - 60 = | |
| 6 | 28 - 7 = | | 28 | 80 - 70 = | |
| 7 | 39 - 8 = | | 29 | 88 - 70 = | |
| 8 | 31 - 2 = | | 30 | 48 - 4 = | |
| 9 | 41 - 3 = | | 31 | 80 - 40 = | |
| 10 | 51 - 4 = | | 32 | 81 - 40 = | |
| 11 | 61 - 5 = | | 33 | 46 - 3 = | |
| 12 | 30 - 9 = | | 34 | 60 - 30 = | |
| 13 | 40 - 8 = | | 35 | 68 - 30 = | |
| 14 | 50 - 7 = | | 36 | 67 - 4 = | |
| 15 | 60 - 6 = | | 37 | 67 - 40 = | |
| 16 | 40 - 30 = | | 38 | 89 - 6 = | |
| 17 | 41 - 30 = | | 39 | 89 - 60 = | |
| 18 | 40 - 20 = | | 40 | 76 - 2 = | |
| 19 | 42 - 20 = | | 41 | 76 - 20 = | |
| 20 | 80 - 50 = | | 42 | 54 - 6 = | |
| 21 | 85 - 50 = | | 43 | 65 - 8 = | |
| 22 | 80 - 40 = | | 44 | 87 - 9 = | |

© Bill Davidson

**B**
Subtract.

Improvement _____    # Correct _____

| | | | | | |
|---|---|---|---|---|---|
| 1 | 43 - 2 = | | 23 | 94 - 50 - | |
| 2 | 55 - 3 = | | 24 | 90 - 60 - | |
| 3 | 67 - 4 = | | 25 | 96 - 60 = | |
| 4 | 79 - 5 = | | 26 | 80 - 70 = | |
| 5 | 89 - 6 = | | 27 | 87 - 70 = | |
| 6 | 98 - 7 = | | 28 | 90 - 80 = | |
| 7 | 29 - 8 = | | 29 | 98 - 80 = | |
| 8 | 21 - 2 = | | 30 | 39 - 4 = | |
| 9 | 31 - 3 = | | 31 | 90 - 40 = | |
| 10 | 41 - 4 = | | 32 | 91 - 40 = | |
| 11 | 51 - 5 = | | 33 | 47 - 3 = | |
| 12 | 20 - 9 = | | 34 | 70 - 30 = | |
| 13 | 30 - 8 = | | 35 | 78 - 30 = | |
| 14 | 40 - 7 = | | 36 | 68 - 4 = | |
| 15 | 50 - 6 = | | 37 | 68 - 40 = | |
| 16 | 30 - 20 = | | 38 | 89 - 7 = | |
| 17 | 31 - 20 = | | 39 | 89 - 70 = | |
| 18 | 50 - 30 = | | 40 | 56 - 2 = | |
| 19 | 52 - 30 = | | 41 | 56 - 20 = | |
| 20 | 70 - 40 = | | 42 | 34 - 6 = | |
| 21 | 75 - 40 = | | 43 | 45 - 8 = | |
| 22 | 90 - 50 = | | 44 | 57 - 9 = | |

© Bill Davidson

Name _____          Date _____

Draw a tape diagram for each step.

1. Maura's ribbon is 26 cm long. Colleen's ribbon is 14 cm shorter than Maura's ribbon. What is the total length of both the ribbons?

   Step 1: Find the length of Colleen's ribbon.

   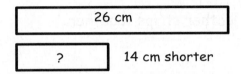

   Step 2: Find the length of both ribbons.

   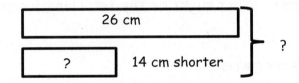

2. Jesse's doll is 30 cm tall. Sarah's doll is 9 cm shorter than Jessie's doll. What is the total length of both dolls?

   Step 1: Find the length of Sarah's doll.

   Step 2: Find the length of both dolls.

3. Steven has a black leather strip that is 13 centimeters long. He cut off 5 centimeters. His teacher gave him a brown leather strip that is 16 centimeters long. What is the total length of both strips?

Step 1: Find the length of black leather strip after being cut.

Step 2: Find the length of the black and brown leather strips together.

4. Pam and Mark measured the distance around each other's wrists. Pam's measured 10 cm. Mark's measured 3 cm more than Pam's. What might be the total length around their wrists (all four wrists).

Step 1: Find the distance around both Mark's wrists.

Step 2: Find the total measurement of all four wrists.

Name _____    Date _____

The length of a crayon is 9 centimeters.  A pencil is 11 centimeters longer than the crayon.  What is the total length of both the crayon and the pencil?

Lesson 10:   Apply conceptual understanding of measurement by solving two-
             step word problems.
Date:        6/26/13

2.D.35

© 2013 Common Core, Inc. All rights reserved. commoncore.org

Name _____ Date _____

Draw a tape diagram for each step.

1. There is 29 cm of green ribbon. A blue ribbon is 9 cm shorter than the green ribbon. How long is the green ribbon?

   Step 1: Find the length of blue ribbon.

   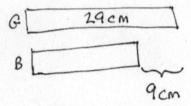

   Step 2: Find the length of both the blue and green ribbons.

   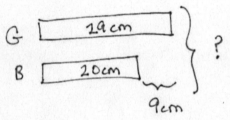

2. Joanna and Lisa drew lines. Joanna's line is 41 cm long. Lisa's line is 19 cm longer than Joanna's. How long are Joanna and Lisa's lines?

   Step 1: Find the length of Lisa's line.

   Step 2: Find the total length of their lines.

COMMON CORE

Lesson 10: Apply conceptual understanding of measurement by solving two-step word problems.
Date: 6/26/13

2.D.36

© 2013 Common Core, Inc. All rights reserved. commoncore.org

Name _____    Date _____

1. Use your ruler to find the length of the pencil and the crayon.

    a.  How long is the crayon? _____ centimeters

    b.  How long is the pencil? _____ centimeters

    c.  Which is longer?       pencil       crayon

    d.  How much longer? _____ centimeters

2. Samantha and Bill are having a bean bag throwing contest and need to measure each of their throws.

a. Circle the most appropriate tool to measure their throws.

    ruler          paper clips                 meter stick          centimeter cubes

b. Explain your choice using pictures or words.

c. Bill throws his bean bag 5 meters, which was 2 meters farther than Samantha threw her bean bag. How far did Samantha throw her bean bag? Draw a diagram or picture to show the length of their throws.

d. Sarah threw her bean bag 3 meters farther than Bill. Who won the contest? How do you know?

3. Use the broken centimeter ruler to solve the problem.

A grasshopper jumped 7 centimeters forward and 4 centimeters back and then stopped. If the grasshopper started at 18, where did the grasshopper stop? Show your work.

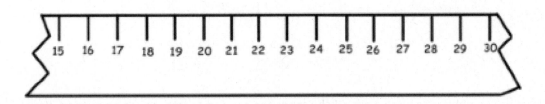

4.

Vanessa's Ribbons

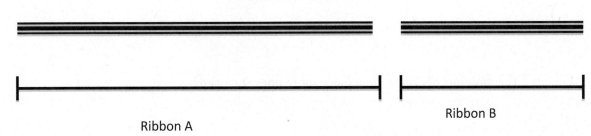

Ribbon A

Ribbon B

a. Measure the length of Ribbon A with your centimeter ruler and your paper clip. Write the measurements on the lines below.

_____centimeters                    _____paper clips

b. Explain why the number of centimeters is larger than the number of paper clips. Use pictures or words.

c.   Estimate the length of Ribbon B in paper clips.

_____paper clips

d.   How much longer is Ribbon A than Ribbon B?  Give your answer in centimeters.

e.   Vanessa is using the ribbons to wrap a gift.  If she tapes the ribbons together with no overlap, how many centimeters of ribbon does she have altogether?

f.   If Vanessa needs 20 centimeters of ribbon, how much more does she need?

**Measure and estimate lengths in standard units.**

**2.MD.1**   Measure the length of an object by selecting and using appropriate tools such as rulers, yardsticks, meter sticks, and measuring tapes.

**2.MD.2**   Measure the length of an object twice, using length units of different lengths for the two measurements; describe how the two measurements relate to the size of the unit chosen.

**2.MD.3**   Estimate lengths using units of inches, feet, centimeters, and meters.

**2.MD.4**   Measure to determine how much longer one object is than another, expressing the length difference in terms of a standard length unit.

**Relate addition and subtraction to length.**

**2.MD.5**   Use addition and subtraction within 100 to solve word problems involving lengths that are given in the same units, e.g., by using drawings (such as drawings of rulers) and equations with a symbol for the unknown number to represent the problem.

**2.MD.6**   Represent whole numbers as lengths from 0 on a number line diagrams with equally spaced points corresponding to the numbers 0, 1, 2, …, and represent whole number sums and differences within 100 on a number line diagram.

## Evaluating Student Learning Outcomes

A Progression Toward Mastery is provided to describe steps that illuminate the gradually increasing understandings that students develop *on their way to proficiency.* In this chart, this progress is presented from left (Step 1) to right (Step 4). The learning goal for each student is to achieve Step 4 mastery. These steps are meant to help teachers and students identify and celebrate what the student can do now, and what they need to work on next.

## A Progression Toward Mastery

| Assessment Task Item | STEP 1 Little evidence of reasoning without a correct answer. (1 Point) | STEP 2 Evidence of some reasoning without a correct answer. (2 Points) | STEP 3 Evidence of some reasoning with a correct answer or evidence of solid reasoning with an incorrect answer. (3 Points) | STEP 4 Evidence of solid reasoning with a correct answer. (4 Points) |
|---|---|---|---|---|
| **1** <br><br> **2.MD.1** <br> **2.MD.4** | The student is unable to answer either question correctly. | The student measures the length of the two objects correctly *or* determines that the pencil is longer. | The student correctly: <br> ▪ Measures the length of the crayon and pencil. <br> ▪ Determines that the pencil is longer. <br> ▪ Makes an error in determining the difference in length. | The student correctly: <br> ▪ Meausres the crayon and the pencil. <br> ▪ Determines that the pencil is longer. <br> ▪ Determines the difference in length between the pencil and crayon. |
| **2** <br><br> **2.MD.1** <br> **2.MD.5** | The student is unable to answer any question correctly. | ▪ The student is not able to choose an appropriate tool for measurement but can accurately depict the two throws with a picture. <br> ▪ Student chooses an appropriate strategy for solving but makes an error in computation. | ▪ The student selects an appropriate tool for measurement but cannot explain why *or* the student selects ruler as the measuring tool. <br> ▪ Student accurately represents the comparison of the throws with a picture. <br> ▪ Correctly identifies contest winner. | The student correctly: <br> ▪ Identifies meter stick as the tool for measurement and defends reasoning. <br> ▪ Student accurately represents the comparison of the throws with a picture. <br> ▪ Correctly identifies contest winner. |
| **3** <br><br> **2.MD.6** | ▪ The student shows no movement on the ruler. <br> ▪ The student is unable to answer the question correctly. | ▪ The student shows only one movement on the ruler. <br> ▪ Student correctly adds 7 but does not subtract 4. | ▪ The student shows only one movement, on the ruler. <br> ▪ Student correctly identifies where the grasshopper stops. | The student correctly: <br> ▪ Uses centimeter ruler as a number line, showing movement forward and backward as adding and subtracting. <br> ▪ Correctly identifies where the grasshopper stops. |

## A Progression Toward Mastery

| 4 2.MD.1 2.MD.2 2.MD.3 2.MD.4 2.MD.5 | The student gets no or one question correct. | The student gets two to three of the six questions correct. | The student: | The student: |
|---|---|---|---|---|
| | | | <ul><li>Correctly measures length of Ribbon A in either centimeters or paper clips.</li><li>Provides an explanation of why there is a larger number of centimeters.</li><li>Makes an error in computation when adding the length of the two ribbons together.</li><li>Miscalculates the difference in length between the two ribbons.</li></ul> | <ul><li>Correctly measures length of Ribbon A in both centimeters and paper clips.</li><li>Provides accurate explanation of why there is a larger number of centimeters.</li><li>Correctly estimates Ribbon B in paper clips.</li><li>Correctly measures Ribbon B key in centimeters.</li><li>Identifies that Ribbon A is 4 longer than Ribbon B.</li><li>Determines total length of both ribbons taped together.</li></ul> |

Module 2:     Addition and Subtraction of Length Units
Date:          6/26/13

2.S.7

Name _____Josh_____          Date _____

1.  Use your ruler to find the length of the pencil and the crayon.

a.  How long is the crayon? ___9___ centimeters

b.  How long is the pencil? ___11___ centimeters

c.  Which is longer?     ⬭pencil⬭          crayon

d.  How much longer? ___2___ centimeters

2. Samantha and Bill are having a bean bag throwing contest and need to measure each of their throws.

a. Circle the most appropriate tool to measure their throws.

ruler          paper clips          (meter stick)          centimeter cubes

b. Explain your choice using pictures or words.

Samantha and Bill threw far and a meter stick is the longest tool.

c. Bill throws his bean bag 5 meters, which was 2 meters farther than Samantha threw her bean bag. How far did Samantha throw her bean bag? Draw a diagram or picture to show the length of their throws.

Bill [ ][ ][ ][ ][ ]
Samantha [ ][ ][ ]

3 meters

d. Sarah threw her bean bag 3 meters farther than Bill. Who won the contest? How do you know?

5 + 3 = 8
Sarah won because 8 is more than 5.

3.  Use the broken centimeter ruler to solve the problem.

A grasshopper jumped 7 centimeters forward and 4 centimeters back and then stopped.  If the grasshopper started at 18, where did the grasshopper stop?  Show your work.

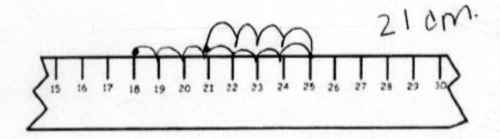

21 cm.

4.

Vanessa's Ribbons

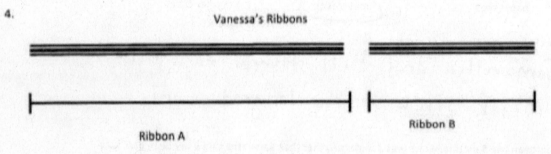

Ribbon A                    Ribbon B

a.  Measure the length of Ribbon A with your centimeter ruler and your paper clip.  Write the measurements on the lines below.

   11 centimeters                    3 paper clips

b.  Explain why the number of centimeters is larger than the number of paper clips.  Use pictures or words.

a paperclip is longer than
a centimeter, so you need
less paperclips.

c. Estimate the length of Ribbon B in paper clips.

___2___ paper clips

d. How much longer is Ribbon A than Ribbon B? Give your answer in centimeters.

$$11 - 5 = 6 \text{ cm}$$

e. Vanessa is using the ribbons to wrap a gift. If she tapes the ribbons together with no overlap, how many centimeters of ribbon does she have altogether?

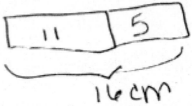

16 cm

f. If Vanessa needs 20 centimeters of ribbon, how much more does she need?

$$20 - 16 = 4 \text{ cm}$$